JUST HEAR ME OUT

AUTHOR | GARI NGUYEN

Who knows what we would be like now if we hadn't dropped our hands on that fateful day—just regular folks with nothing to lose?

___A NOVEL___

GENRE | ROMANCE, THRILLER

The entire novel is a work of fiction.
It's pure chance if it actually exists.

"I confide in my living diary, which is YOU, since no one else gets me.

You're the one who opened my eyes to the fact that other people can view my existence as nothing more than a poor test, though".

Introductory

A young woman with a horrific past that she couldn't forget had a burning desire to become a successful screenwriter.

A young director who had everything except for the belief that love might exist in the real world. When he was 19, he made up his mind to investigate the circumstances surrounding his father's death.

Another man had also discovered genuine love, but he was too safe and constrained by his own expectations to risk it all for the woman he loved.

The past continued to haunt the three of them. Despite this, they continued to encourage themselves to leave everything behind. Even in public, they appeared to be "always fine."

All three meet again at what appeared to be a stable time, but they were all "disrupted" and disturbed when their feelings for each other exceeded the limit.

Was it true, after all, that all pain in the world was caused only by men's and women's love?

SaiGon - December 2017

6.00 PM

"*Grab hold of my hand! Remember! In no event should you let go of my hand*". The mother with the blue yoga pants and white sweater explained it to her little child gently.

"Yes." The kid grinned and held his mom's hand as they played with the Yoyo.

The woman stood in the middle of a red light at a busy Saigon junction and studied the child's face intently. He might be only five years old, but he moved like a grown man. He never questioned her happiness, but he always knew when she was faking it.

While she understood that the child was the result of a mistake she made as a young woman, she couldn't deny that she was richer and more fully experienced because of him.

She was deep in thought when her new employer contacted her via email to schedule a phone interview for a job.

"If I take advantage of this chance, I won't have to stress about money ever again! I'll be able to secure the boy's financial future".

She was often researching fresh information on the company she was going to work for, all the while fantasizing about the large pay she would soon be receiving.

The kid dropped her hand and she didn't even realize it.

"Do not hold back. Strike forcefully! Don't just "stop the game," though, give it a good shake first". The boy was too preoccupied with his final game of Yo-Yo running around the park's perimeter road to stop bouncing along it. The rope snapped and the Yo-yo sailed out into the street, where nobody saw it coming.

The child instinctively went to the middle of the road to retrieve the toy, not realizing that the halo he was about to see from the bus's headlights would be the last he would ever see.

Kttttt..... Rapid deceleration was achieved using the car's brakes. The driver's face was pale because he couldn't identify the object he had struck;

all he knew was that something wasn't right.

A kid, perhaps five years old, was motionless on the road. The Yoyo obeyed his every command and sat quietly by his side.

"This is obviously not the case. Don't just walk away from me. What we're experiencing here is surely only a dream"

The young woman looked up in shock at the sight before her. She hurried over to the kid and cradled him in her arms while she frantically called 911. Her shirt and skirt were stained with blood and tears. The kid, however, was no longer in her care. His wanderings had taken him to a different universe. She could not determine how far away the boy was.

Her eyes welling up, the mother could only brush the eyes of the kid who had never left her side in those five years.

Chapter 1

***

"I'm still the same person I always was, but success in the marketplace and widespread media attention have given me the wherewithal to do the right thing. If you dye your hair, get a new outfit, put on some lipstick and eyeliner, no one will ever know how you really feel. Do you think that anyone even notices you at all? You must always give the impression that everything is perfect for them".

***

December 2012

"When I was younger...
My heart was as pure as my face...
And I loved without any ulterior motives...."

Just as Phuong finished the final step of applying eyeshadow, she sang along to the music playing on her iPod, which was conveniently situated on the vanity mirror. It didn't matter how meticulously she applied this blush in her signature sepia tone; the weariness of the past few days was still visible in her eyes.

Phuong arrived at the company every day at 8 a.m., worked until 10 p.m., then took antidepressants and sleep aids to ensure she didn't deviate from her routine.

Phuong's daily routine had not changed in the five years since she acquired the role of Communications Director at the company behind the most popular Vietnamese messaging app. She had to take significantly more effort than usual to avoid becoming "scattered" in the midst of this intense atmosphere.

Phuong rose earlier than usual this morning. Since she was meeting a VIP, she also applied more cosmetics than usual. She hoped that by making him feel welcome and showing him that she had matured and been very successful in life, he would come to the conclusion that...

... she had indeed lived the life he had wished for her.

This winter was so chilly that the customary "cold" weather of Saigon had to "subdue," so Phuong grinned slightly as she stepped out of the home in a form-fitting black dress and carefully put on her favorite brown coat. She sat in a familiar Porsche and observed the area outside the prison gate, where people were both pleased and sad to see their loved ones again after so many years apart. Some other people were standing alone, unsure of what to do because no one ever asked.

An unexpected chill ran through Phuong's body. Even after all these years, she still has no idea if life is different on the other side of the wall. Phuong's train of thinking was abruptly broken when she spotted a familiar face off in the distance.

An was there. He was the last prisoner out as the doors to the jail opened. The door to his frigid cell shut behind him. Even after all these years, Phuong could still clearly recall An's smile.

"You haven't changed at all!" Phuong leapt out of the car, dashed over to embrace An.

"You've remained the same." And smiled. *"Your hair's length and curliness enhance your beauty." As far as I can tell, you're now the boss."*

"I'm glad you made it back to the free world." As Phuong smiled, tears welled up in her eyes.

***

S. Apartment, District 2

An widened his eyes wide as she came into Phuong's house. In terms of size, Phuong's flat was far too large for her to live comfortably. The space was open and airy, with finely built architecture and a relaxing gray paint color accented with a few small purple orchid pots to relieve stress. The photographs of An and Phuong were tastefully framed and hung on the wall.

An took around 15 minutes to observe Phuong's full residence before settling in the spot where a variety of dishes were laid on the table:

"How long have you been in this place?" An asked Phuong

"Five years have passed since my promotion. I am the company's youngest Director of Communications!"

"Congratulations, Phuong!"

"Thank you!".

"...."

"What makes you happy? Eat rapidly! All of these are my favorite dishes! It's all my cooking." Phuong feigned to make a fist with her hand.

An smiled, quietly appreciating the exquisitely arranged food. An had not experienced the freshness of the food or the purity of the water for a very long time.

While enjoying a delicious meal, An turned around inadvertently and viewed himself in the enormous mirror situated opposite. Short jagged hair, tanned skin a lot. The clothing that An was wearing had not been washed properly and were rather ragged because he had been wearing them since the day she entered prison over ten years ago.

After hearing An said, "Thank God you escaped that location early... I've been waiting for you," Phuong looked in the mirror and let go of An's words. She saw reflections of herself and An there, as clear as they had been 10 years before.

An buried his feelings by burying his face in the rice plate and eating till he nearly choked. Phuong checked the time and comforted An by placing a hand on his shoulder.

"Today, my partner and I have a very crucial appointment. Let's catch up later tonight. Have at your leisure anything in the home".

Aware of how challenging it was for the two of them to resume their previous level of conversation, An smiled and finished his meal in silence.

An quickly noticed that Phuong was missing something essential: the girl who used to joke around, chatter nonstop, and openly display her attitude. Instead, there were powdered eyes and dark red lips on a face that looked ruddy. Now, An had no idea what the former friend was thinking.

***

Phuong checked the time. There was still no trace of Mac at about 8 p.m. Phuong continued to meet him at X cafe across from the park near his residence. The establishment was still the same, and the menu featured the same drinks and dishes. Phuong regretted that it had been over five years since her last visit to this location. Phuong recalled Mac criticizing this coffee shop for serving the worst rice dish he had ever had in Saigon. Although she disagreed, Phuong simply laughed it off.

Phuong had been unable to stop her heart from gravitating toward Mac for many years. He had a tall frame, weirdly curling hair, smooth white skin, and incredibly alluring soft lips; he was certainly the type of partner that every woman... desired

She recalled thinking that Mac was her life's "marshal" from the moment they first met. She felt a childlike excitement in her chest at that same instant. The man taught her the value of loving someone unconditionally, even if it meant nothing in the end.

"Right! After five years apart, we finally meet again".

Suddenly, Phuong cracked a smile. Phuong would never forget the impact of that unadulterated love on her life at age 22. It was an unexpected display of affection that she pretended to suppress. Phuong believed that, in many cases, it was not that people simply couldn't forget their first love, but rather that they regretted the sensations so deeply that they knew for certain they could never come back.

Mac arrived in front of Phuong, dressed politely in gray and sported a bright smile behind his glasses. She could tell how tired he was just by looking at him. He appeared to be engulfed by grief and shame. Why was he putting so much pressure on his shoulders? She didn't get it.

Still the same sensation, the sensation of the heart racing quicker than normal and the eyes welling up with tears. Phuong remembered her love from five years ago as if it were yesterday. People had told Phuong that these weird sentiments only occurred in front of the person she truly loved. After more than 15 minutes of silence, Phuong spoke out, turning the coffee cup in her palm.

"Are you surprised after living in the UK for a few years and then returning to Vietnam?"

"Haha, what surprise? I prefer to be in Vietnam. Everything has become a lot nicer. But you look so different now!"

Mac's statements elicited no response from Phuong. The dialogue ceased once more. Mac abruptly stated:

"I returned to Vietnam three months ago... I'm married already. I and Ly will be living in Saigon this time."

"3 months ago? So you're trying to avoid me?"

"I'm at a loss for words because I ran into you again."

"Do you still have a lot to do with this city?"

"I have not anticipated this day. I also told you to come here to start a business before, right?"

"Yes. More opportunities, easier to live in Saigon!"

Phuong was laughing, but deep inside she was unhappy. The sight of the gold ring on his finger made her gasp.

After he left for England to pursue his master's degree, she did not get in touch with Mac again for a very long time. As things stood, however, she found herself at a loss for words. Maybe it was not the story they were telling each other that was the issue, but the fact that they were so far apart that their conduct couldn't go back to the minute it all started.

She was the first to have feelings for Mac five years ago, and she was also the one to finally put an end to their doomed relationship. When Phuong looked at him, he saw a respectable man who seemed content with his life. She freely admitted that she was self-centered. How could she bestow a blessing on someone she still cared about?

She didn't give a damn about how noble anyone else was. So, love entails giving without expecting anything in return? Was that what we call "real love"? Was that the case? Wasn't that merely the loser's excuse?

As much as she desired him, he was still over a thousand and seven hundred and thirty five kilometer distance away. She woke up one morning still lonely and alone, the same figure he had been in all her dreams. Since she had witnessed him with another woman, she had no grounds on which to compete for his attention.

It was clear that he had Phuong's undying affection. It was not something he was unaware of. However, Mac already had a girlfriend at the time, and this was likely what led him to reject Phuong. But what could he do? Phuong's heart had already given by the time he finally spoke it.

***

After spending almost an hour chatting quietly with Mac, Phuong decided to head home. As soon as she walked inside, she grabbed a cotton pad to wipe off her makeup. As she leaned against the sink, staring at herself in the glass, she had the distinct impression that she was looking back in time five years, to the day she turned 22.

Phuong was still the same. What made her who she was now couldn't be changed.

She was 27 years old and had nothing to show for it except wrinkles on her forehead, depression, and frizzy hair. Phuong's calm demeanor, smile, and well-kept hair were the kindest aspects of her professional appearance.

Mac was really special to Phuong. Whether she retained the object of her affection or not, the intensity of her feelings for it remained the same as the day they first met.

"Without parting ways that day, who would they be now?"

Phuong became buried in a sea of ideas. Her thoughts turned to the question of why people got married and stayed together for so long if love existed but coudn't last forever.

"Is it fate that two people who have waited so long for each other finally find each other in love?"

Phuong got in the tub and filled it as high as it would go. She desperately wished she could stay submerged in the soothing water indefinitely. When I said that, Phuong chuckled. The eyes burned and the heart ached, but the meaned to alleviate those discomforts were out of reach.

Phuong hid her face from view. She jumped as she heard the bathroom door creak opened. She didn't turn it off, but the water pressure in the faucet eventually dropped. When she finally opened her eyes, she noticed a young boy, perhaps around five years old, standing next to her and smiling broadly. It looked like someone had tied her up since her body was completely rigid. She was at a loss for words and could only stare at him.

The boy was dressed in her old white pullover and her favorite pair of comfortable blue tracksuit trousers.

He said nothing and simply stared at her. The boy smiled automatically as he gently waved the Yoyo in front of her. She had just reached out her hand to touch the boy's face when the figure vanished.

Knock knock...

"Are you all right? You've been in the shower for over an hour!" An inquired.

"Not a problem! I'm perfectly fine." Phuong fought to keep the trembling at bay.

"Just let me know if you need anything!" Phuong's thoughts were interrupted when An's voice came from outside the bathroom door.

"Don't be concerned! Go to bed first!" Phuong responded.

Phuong closed her eyes and continued to relax in the water after quickly smoking a couple medicinal marijuana cigarettes. At times like these, she wished to be immersed in an endless dream, never to awaken.

The night was always lonely for her, but it was also when she felt the most at peace. Because the best part about being alone was that no one else could ever hurt her.

***

After a few random lines, An closed the diary. He collapsed on the bed after a long day. Despite the fact that this was his first day out of prison, his mood hadn't improved much. He felt lonely and abandoned during his time in prison, and he still faced a slew of challenges ahead.

An had to learn how to fight to survive since the day he was imprisoned, day by day, month by month, year by year. It was all he could do to save her own life.

An realized he would have to suffer rejection from people no matter what his career when he was fortunate enough to be granted amnesty from that torment. He nevertheless agreed to do it once again. Anyone would not readily trust someone with a criminal history, so that made sense, right?

An, who was lying next to Phuong, turned to face her and was about to speak to her when he noticed that she was asleep. Anyone's shift was inevitable, An realized as he examined Phuong's face in the yellow light, tracing each line on her face. But in front of the person they loved, they remained the same as when they first met, regardless of how much their looks had changed or how strong they had become. Phuong was still very vulnerable with An. All emotions—sad, happy, and otherwise—were still communicated in full clarity.

An appeared to be dreaming as he laid next to Phuong after many years apart. He never expected to be able to see every line on her face so vividly. An, like Phuong, seems to be the suspicious type. *"Love someone even if you were only looking from afar? It was quite noble! Why not take advantage of the opportunity to be close, because that person's feelings may also change?"*

An softly kissed Phuong on the lips. That kiss was brief, but it was enough to wake Phuong up and push An away. An drew a sigh from Phuong. Despite the fact that she wasn't astonished, she quickly turned her back to evade as a retort.

An turned to face the opposite window, smiling. Tonight, the moon was still unusually bright.

The moon was just as dazzling ten years earlier on that night. Unfortunately, the faint light transformed his life into a whole other set of days, filled with nothing but silent agony and loneliness.

Chapter 2

***

*"Not because I don't love you
but because that love was insufficient to convince me to stay."*

***

Khanh took a big breath of the exotic air in Saigon as he stood in the centre of the airport. It had been over a year since he left to study overseas and he was finally back in Hanoi.

Hanoi made him feel at ease, yet it was unable to satisfy his desires. He was no longer able to fall asleep thinking about his beautiful childhood and loving family. Time for him to make his mark in the entertainment industry by expanding his brand. To pursue his goals, he boldly set off for the South.

Khanh was confused as to why he felt compelled to visit Saigon. For Saigon was not nearly as wonderful as he had assumed, but it nevertheless made him addicted in ways he hadn't yet to fully comprehended.

He was sitting in a cab, getting ready to head back to the house he had purchased in Saigon two years prior, when he broke out into a broad grin. It was once his fondest hope, but now that his family was broken, he found the idea laughable.

Khanh and his mother were abandoned by their father. When he was 19 years old, he left for a distant land. His father was the producer of one of Hanoi's most successful film companies, and the family had lived comfortably off of his father's wealth. However, after his father's untimely death, the family was forced to declare bankruptcy. Then he and his mom had to figure out how to get back to their old life, which meant going back to basics.

The press "brainwashed" the people that day into believing that his father was killed in a random act of robbery and murder at his Saigon house. Still, he didn't buy it. His father had studied martial arts, so he was prepared for any threat; however, the perpetrator that year turned out to be an orphaned girl who looked precisely like a boy and was severely addicted to meth. Wouldn't her recklessness increase if the only motivation was financial gain? Because ultimately she received a severe sentence that landed her in prison.

Khanh didn't want to give up so easily. He was determined to learn the truth about his father's death. He intended to find the guilty again that year. To investigate. To torment. To confirm and believe that something was true. But he had no idea where to begin. He was not led by anyone. He could only trust his heart and intuition.

Khanh felt indescribably sad when he suddenly remembered the past. It turned out that the crisis era, during which he attempted to obtain a bank loan to study directing in France, had ended. The time when he attempted to invest in filmmaking with his pals and was turned down. The period in which he shown no calm, did not even ponder, and simply raced into the hazards of life.

There had been mistakes and accomplishments, and he was now the first Vietnamese director to win the prestigious French César prize, something that not everyone his age could do. Khanh's career had taken off like a kite in the wind since that milestone two years ago. He was the owner of Huy Khanh Film Studio, which he named after himself and had offices in Saigon and Hanoi. He built a house, acquired a car, and lived a solitary life surrounded by several girls.

It sounded like he was happy, but Khanh never thought he was.

Through the taxi window, Khanh viewed the sights and sounds of Saigon. It was a mystery why so many beautiful Saigon women look the same. Khanh had difficulty developing romantic feelings. In an instant, Khanh thought back to Minh Ngoc, the girl he had a serious crush on when he was only 19 and a half years old. The one for whom he once sacrificed everything just to maintain her approval. She was also the reason Khanh could no longer love anyone with his whole heart.

This void had worn him down emotionally and physically. If modern women had become so nasty and forgetful, why was that? How come modern-day women had it so easy in the love department? Why were women always so alike?

In Khanh's mind, Minh Ngoc's words remained fresh. The best way to move on from each other, she added, was to avoid becoming friends or even exchanging words. Not because she found Khanh's messages unpleasant or boring, but because she genuinely wanted what was best for him.

However, she was unaware that Khanh was extremely adept at absorbing other people's words. Khanh would grin and silently leave her life if she asked him to be quiet. Khanh vowed to himself that he would never return to Minh Ngoc.

Khanh arrived home and looked out the window at the Saigon rain. Khanh swiped the screen, picking a few girls on Tinder - an app that was still "renowned" for being used to find "one-night stands" and "love-without-binding" relationships. It was unfortunate that he inadvertently selected a few people that had the same appearance, hair, lips, and smile as Minh Ngoc. When he woken up next to an unfamiliar female, he wondered to himself, *"Why is my taste in women so simple? Why do I keep doing this succession of days?"* Although, in his heart, he told himself it was just a means to release stress, a chance to make his life more colorful after a long day at work.

Khanh had lost faith and didn't need anything intangible and unquantifiable like love. He only needed a few girls to hang out with, converse with, make love with, and sleep with. Khanh might be pragmatic, but he never used the term "love" to trick females into sleeping with him; Khanh lord loathed such vile men. After all, even after six or seven years of dating, people may still split up, let alone Khanh, who was just a regular guy with flaws. Was there any love capable of rescuing Khanh...

The sky went black, and small beads of water clung to Khanh's hair.

Saigon greeted Khanh once more in an unflattering manner. Khanh's feelings had not changed despite the passage of more than a year. Saigon had never made him feel at ease, but it had never fooled him, never made him feel as painful and depressing as the days in Hanoi.

***

9.am. Khanh walked into the studio wearing a crisp white shirt, dark slacks, and his trusty Sony headphones. He liked this "manly" image for a long time, even though he didn't have to dress seriously; he could wear this magnificent attire wherever he chose. Khanh liked listening to gentle music, particularly known old tunes. Khanh only wanted to live in the past, and didn't care what anyone said. They had no idea what Khanh had gone through.

Khanh drew all eyes from the moment they stepped into the elevator to the moment they arrived at the office, thanks to his narrow black specs and meticulously maintained white skin. Khanh seemed uninterested, instead continuing to swipe through a few Tinder profiles with his hand to "start" the morning as usual.

"Ting". The elevator's sound indicated that it had arrived on the 9th floor. *"After a morning of horrendous traffic, I was finally able to arrive"*. Khanh raised his head.

Khanh had just walked out of the elevator when he was unexpectedly bumped into a strange woman with a cup of hot coffee in her hand, putting a few stains on her clothing. Khanh simply looked up at the woman and mumbled, "Sorry!" before disappearing. The woman was taken aback, and all she could do was shrug and shake her head at this somewhat disrespectful and uncaring man. It wouldn't help if she cursed or made a big fuss about it now that the key meeting was approaching.

Khanh was sitting at his workstation when he noticed the HR staff at the other table winking at him. He grinned. Khanh was passionate about his work. Khanh was fond of women. Khanh, on the other hand, did not believe in love. He wasn't ready to commit to anyone and simply wanted to have some fun. After all, romantic love only provided happiness for a few brief moments, not a lifetime. It was alright to claim Khanh had no heart, that he had run out of love, if Khanh had ever grasped what true love was.

"Hello. Here's a list of scripts to think about at this afternoon's discussion. Examine it out!" The assistant, who wore thick glasses and had curly hair, smiled warmly as if to impress Khanh.

"I'm grateful. Just give it to me, please." Khanh answered casually while keeping his face pressed against the computer screen. He was aware that he did not regard his subordinates with disdain, but he was unable to interact with them in a kind manner.

The assistant stood there staring at Khanh for a considerable amount of time, appearing somewhat helpless due to her excess. She lowered her face and silently departed the space, expecting him to "summon" her when necessary.

Khanh was still unconcerned with her opinion of him. Did he really need to appear thrilled when he was completely emotionless? *"It all came down to how you live"*.

He detested the phrase "deep acting" the most: *"Don't let people see your sentiments!"* Why did you feel the need to exaggerate and complicate something that was simply life? Khanh didn't enjoy hiding, and he didn't appear to be cool. All that had changed was that Khanh was still there.

***

Ha sighed, frustrated. Her previous bosses had the same mood swings. Now, boss Phuong - the woman who always appeared serious - had just given her a thrashing for a minor error in the report this morning. Everyone thought a recent graduate like Ha could only be a runner, nothing more, nothing less.

Even though she began working at the age of 18, Ha was unable to attain her goals no matter how hard she worked. What happened in life that *"becoming rich isn't that difficult"* or *"just be yourself, why think"*, as the media or exhortations suggest.

Ha gradually developed a habit of boring, safe existence. She didn't know when, Ha was too used to living at the office like a "woman" in a meaningless way: spending a lot of money on designer bags, clothes, and shoes. She still ate quick noodles, tinned meat, and a few bottles of cheap fruit drinks in the evening.

To be accepted in a community, she sought to adapt, imitate, and live the manner of others. But she never felt like she fit in this tumultuous and scrutinized office

Ha was 22 years old, the age of a recent graduate, simply lived in such disarray. Living each day knowing that day, carefree and liberal, was how she made others like her, but it had also caused her many problems.

Ha enjoyed singing and hoped to perform in front of a large crowd one day, but she couldn't stake her life on a hobby without a solid basis. So, while it was unknown how long she would work in the office, her singing career had never begun.

"Stop fantasizing and start being more practical!". Ha reflected to herself.

The phone rang, and Ha was startled out of her reverie. Ha returned to work, having drank the last of the unfinished cup of black coffee. She started working like a machine every day.

Ha knew what she had to do every morning when she got up.

How long had it been since she finished her favorite novel or spent some time practicing ukulele music?

It had been a long time since she had naturally woken up early or had been so engrossed in something that she couldn't sleep.

***

"If no one has an opinion, I'd want to end the meeting for the day!"

Phuong finished presenting the product's new media strategy. She smiled as everyone exited the meeting room, though she was still disturbed by the yellow coffee stain on her shirt made by the weird man in the elevator this morning.

Phuong was quietly moving paperwork when she noticed a text message informing her that her appointment with Mac was on the 52nd floor of the Bitexco building. She unintentionally smiled. Mac's birthday was today. He scheduled a meeting with her so that they could both have more time to discuss.

Sometimes, she didn't understand why he wanted to visit her again at this time. What was the cause other than that he simply hadn't forgotten her yet? Or was there something else he wanted to rely on her for? Before, too, no matter how much she loved him, there were still hidden corners, the calculations in Mac that Phuong, no matter how hard she tried, could not see through and could not understand.

Mac and her were, after all, just a desperate relationship. Although, unconsciously since the age of 22, she still felt that he was the guy of her life: the person she was continually looking for, the person she dared to exhibit even the worst sides of her nature. But obviously, he still couldn't love her the way he loved his wife.

The appointment was still 30 minutes away! To pass the time while waiting for the elevator at the company's offices, Phuong opened Tinder again and excitedly swiped her hands a few times. What was she looking for exactly? Was it a friend? Whatever it was, she just wanted to be with that person when she needed to and share something with them, and that was enough for her. Who had time to be in a meaningful relationship right now? She was nevertheless aware of how much work remained to be done.

The things that people think were vital for someone, such as protection, concern, and tenderness, were not the only reasons for her existence.

"Ting". As soon as the elevator door opened, Phuong was confronted with the man she had met earlier that day.

"It was him once more!" Phuong entered the elevator, cursing in her stomach.

"I apologize for this morning... "I was in a rush!" Khanh expressed regret.

"Nothing. It's also due to my quickness." Without looking at Khanh, Phuong responded.

The elevator bell rung, indicating that it had arrived at the ground floor. Phuong walked away harshly. It also appeared to be a touch of fate, didn't it? Khanh thought to himself, chuckling at her infantile demeanor.

***

Mac sat in the high chair of the EON 52 Heli Bar on the 52nd floor of the Bitexco building. Five years ago, he and Phuong sat at this bar all night just to talk. It was also the time when he was the joyful. Phuong was only 22 at the time. And now, at the age of 32, he had outlived her. Age has allowed both of them to mature and recognize what they should and should not do.

While on a business trip to Hanoi, Mac met Phuong for the first time, and he was instantly smitten. She was tall and lean with broad shoulders and ample breasts, and her high cheekbones, straight nose, and soft eyes gave her an air of undeniable fragility. Just by talking to her, he was certain that any man would quickly "fall down" by that peculiar attraction, even though she was neither as hot as a hotgirl nor as lovely as a beauty queen. But sadly, that emotion returned to him at a time when his beloved was by his side.

Mac was aware that it wasn't because he didn't love Phuong, but because his feelings for her weren't strong enough to keep him in the relationship. He still had ties to Hanoi through his family and professional obligations. Ly was still holding out hope that he would finally propose. If Phuong was the only reason she encouraged Mac to travel to Saigon and start again, then Mac lacked the guts to make the necessary sacrifice.

No of how he felt, he had to acknowledge Phuong's sincerity. Mac didn't buy the women's common suspicion that it was false. He was willing to take a risk only when he knew he was improving the other person's life in some way.

Mac experienced a mixture of emotions that day, including laughter, excitement, and despair, all brought on by Phuong's initiative in sending a message to show her love for him despite the distance of 1735 kilometers. In his heart of hearts, Mac realized that just because he had the ability to help Phuong didn't mean he should. Her approving feelings, to provide just one example.

It was a dilemma about distance, differences in thinking, Phuong's goal, and his calculation between him and Phuong.

Despite his rejection, Phuong continued to speak, not expecting anything more. She did not abandon her emotions or carry grudges. Everyone assumed she was the third person in the relationship between him and Ly because of him, but the person who was not obvious in this relationship was Mac.

After all, humans were all selfish. Because of a woman, he couldn't establish a reputation as a cheat. After all, it was not easy to live in Hanoi.

"Say I love you again
Perhaps the rain won't stop
The black sweater
Where is it hidden?
Then just let the memories stop there forever"

(*) "Black Sweater" lyrics – Jay Chou

Mac drank the glass of wine on the table while singing along to the music. Although his vision was hazy, he noticed Phuong coming. Mac gazed at the woman in front of him. Behind sharp spectacles and curling chestnut brown hair, she was still the sly girl. Phuong was considerably more gorgeous than previously, and she now had a career and plans for the future. Was there any reason for her to be interested in a regular, married man like him?

"Congratulations on your birthday! What more can you want from me now that you have everything?" Phuong posed a few odd questions to Mac. She wasn't sure what kind of hope or affirmation she expected from him.

"Thank you so much. I'm just regular."

Mac attempted to smile. The smile was nice yet a little forced. His gleaming eyes revealed something profound. It was a little depressing.

Mac could still smell old scents wafting from Phuong's side of the cold bar. Her sensitivity and warmth remained, but the two had little in common. The chasm between them had grown so wide that it felt impossible for him to bridge in order to approach her again.

There were far too many details about her life that he couldn't possibly know, and he had no right to demand that they be revealed. Because she realized, everyone had secrets that couldn't be touched.

"Would you make a different decision if I met you earlier that day?"

"I am perfectly aware that if I could travel back in time, nothing would change. You've got your reasons."

"…"

"Don't worry, you're a pretty girl. I'm aware that many people desire to follow you. However, these days you're wearing a lot of makeup and going for a striking look!"

"..."

"It's not true, I know, but the truth is that I miss you".

The words Mac said left Phuong speechless.

"Wouldn't things be different today if you had said this sentence five years ago?"

Phuong always found it tough to face Mac. He eliminated the chilly, obstinate mentality that she displayed at work every day.

To dry the water that was subtly trickling down her cheek, Phuong used her hand. Naturally, she had missed him and felt incredibly alone without him for the last five years. She was slightly warmed by his remarks, albeit this was unwarranted.

It turned out that while love could be abandoned at that very moment, it couldn't be forgotten.

Chapter 3

*"When you're in love, don't blame people for betraying you;
blame yourself for not being able to look attentively."*

***

10 years ago...

8.00 PM - January 7th 2002

The small girl, dressed in a white sweater and blue athletic shorts, sat alone in the cafe. She was wrapped in a thin layer of garments. It was raining harder than she had anticipated outside. She had no idea why she was sitting here.

Phuong couldn't believe it had just been a week since her father had abandoned her. Her eyes continued to hurt and taste nasty. Her memories of her father were as fresh as yesterday. The one who had just taken her hand in his. The one who was still chastising her for skipping meals the night before. The one kept an eye on her to see if she slept early, stayed up late reading a book, or insisted on watching a few fascinating flicks on her phone.

Phuong's entire body was covered in goosebumps. She didn't want to go back in time like this.

"Phuong, other than being poor, you have nothing to do with poverty!"

Phuong burst out laughing. She was 17 years old. Only one body. There are no parents. There is no money. Helpless. She moved from Quang Nam to Saigon to work in a bar, where she met numerous difficulties.

She caught the attention of everyone from playboys to crazed old guys since she was young, gorgeous, and had an innocent appearance. But they wanted her body any way they could. They were unconcerned about her feelings. They also made no promises to her.

Somehow, just as she had lost all trust and confidence in herself, a woman claiming to be her mother's friend emerged at this dingy pub. Her mother and this woman, both of whom she had no previous recall or impression of.

Lam was the name of her mother. Her mother abandoned her when she was only two or three years old, when she was too little to understand anything. She had forgotten her mother's face, her mother's occupation, and what her mother had confided in her. Her father first revealed to her when she was 17 years old, after her father died of stomach cancer, that her mother was a "prostitute" - a job that the entire society loathed. Regardless of what people said, Dad still loved his mother.

The woman who arrived at the bar offered her a coffee date, claiming to be her mother's friend and living a block away. She had known Phuong since Phuong was a child, back in Quang Nam. She had always wanted to find a way to give back to herself and her family. Because, back when her mother and she were still "practicing," when she was jealously beaten to death by his wife, her mother came to her aid and was fatally stabbed by the gangster. Her mother abandoned her from that day forward. And that woman couldn't forget her mother's affection, partly because she was overwhelmed with gratitude, and partly because she had mistakenly liked her mother as a lover.

She introduced Phuong to a man, a rich man with a lot of money, who could help her move out of her helpless life without having to... "trade off" too much.

Phuong consented to accept her "assistance." She was not wise enough at the moment to suspect or expect anything. Nor did she realize that money would never fall from the sky and be given to no one, nor would there be salvation without sacrifice.

Phuong was waiting for a man in an empty cafe. She was assured that this individual would "assist" her. She might think about it whether it was good or terrible, whatever it took. She didn't have a choice for the time being.

Late at night, as the chilly wind mixed with the rain, a stranger's breath approached Phuong from behind, making her apprehensive. Even though she was warm, she was shivering weirdly. She had no idea what was in store for her in front of her eyes.

She returned her gaze. It was an elderly man from Hanoi. He was in his late forties, dressed in a very respectable suit, and the scent of costly perfume began to permeate her nose. His keen eyes appeared to want to peer into her soul. He presented himself as Huy Khiem, a producer at Hanoi's second largest film company.

From the first time they met, he couldn't provide the impression of trust. But if she and this man were just a money-for-powder relationship with certain principles, why did she have to be so concerned? Whatever occurred, it would happen at some point.

The man spoke little to her. He simply smoked a few cigarettes, sipped his harsh coffee, and periodically turned to stare at her thoughtfully. *What game was he trying to get her into?*

From a social standpoint, education, personality, and interests, she and he had nothing in common. He was the product of a privileged background, whereas she was just a street girl hanging out. Maybe he didn't want to talk to her because she was both illiterate and "poor." He didn't even ask for her. He offered to give her a lot of money if she went with him, did what he wanted, and stayed with him when she could.

Phuong wasn't sure what she could do to aid him, as long as she could work for him and make money. That was all she needed right now.

Phuong didn't understand it till she looked him in the eyes and nodded as a sign that her life had changed. But who knew, she couldn't let go of what she desired.

***

That year, when he was only 19 years old, Khanh applied immediately to the Ho Chi Minh City Procuracy's investigation agency, as well as to have his father's autopsy reports returned by the Forensic Examination Council. He couldn't believe the perpetrator could harm his father in such a terrible and inhumane manner. An ashtray struck his father's skull around 5-7 times.

Khanh was unable to stand that year when he saw the last vestiges of the case. Khanh went to wipe the lingering tears with his hand as he drove home. Khanh could only talk around his mother's enquiries about the situation over the phone. If his mother saw that, she would be surprised and might do something stupid. Khanh appears to be sufficient. He didn't want to lose the person he cared about again. If he had already experienced life's injustices, why couldn't the worst happen again?

"Boom..." The sound of cars colliding was like a thunderclap in the middle of Hanoi's main street. Khanh didn't know what else to do, but the sky became as black as ink in his eyes. Covering injuries and scrapes following a fight makes no sense. When a motorcycle and a truck crashed, he heard the booming of medical car sirens and the muttering of points.

He imagined his life would come to an end in such manner.

He mistook the miracle for something else.

Unexpectedly, a new life has found him since that day.

He came to Saigon ten years later, grateful for the ability to realize what breath was. He chosen to forego the ostensibly serene existence of the present in order to find salvation in his own soul.

Khanh clutched his head with both hands. Khanh believed that his father was always with him and would bless him so that he could learn the truth.

"Do they think an apology would suffice? To be "punished" by being confined to a small space for a few short years?

Certain. Never in my life will I forget what they did to me.

Certain. I will teach them the meaning of suffering".

***

December 2012

Khanh opened his eyes and got out of bed after being inebriated the night before. Anyway, on the first day he arrived at the Southern office, he was so loved and welcomed by his coworkers that it felt like a blessing.

After turning off the phone's alarm, Khanh opened Facebook and noticed Minh Ngoc's photo status on the newsfeed. She was still the girl with the long colorful floral dress on the beach. Minh Ngoc's memories never seemed to disappear in his head.

But he knew he couldn't go back and trust her again. A sourness and wrath welled up within him.

He was learning to sew up his own heart. Whether Khanh attempted to continue missing or hopes, all he received was nothingness.

"In this world, there are performers who perform plays and spectators who watch plays. If the secret love between the two of us is a drama that no one is watching, why keep it going? I left you because I wanted you to be happy." On the day Minh Ngoc departed Khanh, she said this. She came to him swiftly and then left him just as quickly.

"Lie! I love you, not acting, I also didn't want to comprehend the ridiculous fact "separation is for each other"!" Khanh loathed her, but because

he had given her so much love, he couldn't do anything except let her slide out of his grip. In the time since, Khanh changed. He became a person that not Minh Ngoc had ever known.

Now, Khanh was very cautious about entering someone's environment. He didn't let anyone approach him easily.

When he had feelings for someone, Khanh didn't like to make pledges, the promise he made was foolish, time consuming and unreliable at all. He didn't want to mention love, it seemed unreal and weighty. When Khanh was acclimated to the scent of women's skin even in the absence of affection, he wondered if he still had that feeling.

As a famous director, and the owner of a huge film company that was being handled by many investors, there were many ladies surrounding Khanh, he didn't need to think about it, as long as he wanted to, there would be women. Khanh was averse to fitting himself into a predetermined mold.

Khanh could only smile at himself at times. No one believed him because he trusted no one. Khanh had no idea such a thing as love existed; would anyone volunteer to give him such a rare item? *"Love is a sham,"* Khanh said. He was tired of being compelled to form bonds with others. *"Why make promises that an unromantic man like him can't keep?"*

Tinder sent him a message. Khanh stepped forward. This face appeared to be strangely familiar. The girl from yesterday happened to run into Khanh in the elevator.

Avatar was also lovely. But he had no idea why she had liked him on Tinder.

Khanh was intrigued by her behavior, even though he couldn't recall why he had "swipe right" automatically with this female. But that was good because Khanh's goal for using Tinder was not love, but rather a little fun to relieve tension. If the girl was also interested in Khanh, he was willing to accommodate her.

After a few phrases, Khanh understood that this girl was not as horrible as he had feared. Her name turned out to be Phuong. She was also tough, direct, and concise. She stated that she only required a friend and that she did not require the so-called "real love." Khanh started a morning cigarette, half-smiling.

Khanh now had a new hobby after a period of loneliness and boredom. Why not go on a new dating adventure? Why should he invest in love? For him, love was ultimately a game of gain and loss, with both sides calculating their demands, bribery, power, and seduction to satisfy each other's egos.

Unless it was pure love, there was no calculation or desire with Khanh. But he was tired of it. That feeling had almost little possibility of surviving in his head any longer.

He desired to offer as well as receive. He was no longer the clown and unconditional lover he once was. He requested permission to refuse anything that could harm him. Life didn't let him be stupid and sacrifice everything the way he used to.

The music on the radio in Khanh's apartment resounded, as if his heart was still not as cold as he had declared.

"Have you ever seen the eyes of a person in love?
You were warm in my heart
Your scent was like a blossomed flower
I hope for forever, I want your heart
Tonight will never change
Hold my hand
An eternal love will start"... (*)

(*) Lyrics "X-out" song.

***

2012 December

Saigon, X restaurant on the 50th floor of the Y building

1.00 PM

Phuong was sitting at a table by herself at the restaurant, directly across from a window. From this vantage point, she was able to view the sequence of cars following one another, as well as the never-ending stream of people jammed into the lane.

"I can know the size of your clothes,
but I have no idea what the size of your heart is?

Phuong swayed slightly when she rotated the Ipod in her hand. She forgot about life every time she had to ponder stressfully by plugging in headphones and turning on music.

So far, no matter how her life had hanged or how wasteful she had become, Phuong had never forgotten the good old days. Her father's motorbike profession raised her to study for ten years. Before social difference formed a barrier between father and son, Phuong saw his father as a "hero."

She abandoned her father's presence when she was 17 years old, when he was at the school gate waiting to pick her up from school. She pretended she didn't notice, as if she didn't know. She used to think her father's profession as a motobike driver was a cheap thing. The way he spoke and acted indicated that she was ashamed of the countryside. For the first time in her life, she recognized her father's affection for her as impolite and odd, and she desired to be free of that loving hug.

Phuong, on the other hand, secretly liked her father and couldn't deny: he skillfully "raised the rooster alone." He didn't have a diploma, but he had an unbreakable affection. Even the top classes might not have grasped what he was teaching her. "Life was like a desert, only if you went to the end of the sand dunes would you know what happened," he explained. You would learn the essence of the problem if you went carefully and persistently."

Phuong's eyes welled up with tears as she remembered that last sentence. Stomach cancer had taken her life in an instant. Her love for her father came to her thoughts when she was far away from her birthplace, only hearing his voice over the phone, but what else could she do but embrace the memories?

She lost the man she loved the most when she was 17, was abandoned by her grandmother, and discovered the truth about her mother's background as a prostitute, which she had always envisioned in her dreams every night.

She didn't want her life to be predetermined and bleak at the age of 17. When she left Quang Nam and arrived in Saigon, she realized she had a new chance to reinvent herself. She was walking by herself.

Phuong had just completed lunch when she took out her notebook and scribbled down a few lines of her sentiments. Phuong avoided sharing her emotions with others because she believed that everyone would not comprehend what she was saying. She, too, didn't know where to begin because complaining wasn't her strong suit. Only that individual understood the sadness. *"Outsiders, no matter how sympathetic, remain outsiders"*.

Her fingers brushed on the notebook paper. She hadn't kept a diary in a long time. Except for her father, no one knew she had a strong interest in writing. Phuong began writing scripts, creating comics, and hiding them for herself at the age of nine and ten, after seeing movies. Phuong gradually learned what she enjoyed. She enjoyed the stories and the narrative. She aspired to be the "coolest" screenwriter in Hollywood. That had nothing to do with a young lady like Phuong. She was lovely, she had ambitions, and she was capable. She simply lacked the necessary people to help her dream become a reality.

Despite becoming the youngest Communications Director of the present technology group at the age of 27, Phuong still felt like an outsider in the midst of Saigon's urban life when she acquired a high-class condo in Saigon.

Her goal was as lengthy as the line of cars outside the window. Was it because her current employment was only a means to an end of "rice-clothes-rice-money," because her dream of becoming a famous screenwriter couldn't be realized, or because Saigon had never felt like home to her? However, due to her practical and chilly personality, Phuong was forced to temporarily put that ambition in the back of her mind, forcing herself to create talents to adapt to the times.

Unconsciously, Phuong reflected on An. She was at a loss for words when confronted with An these days. She had an unending pain in her heart everytime she thought about how he faced all the sufferings in the prison. She felt her personality was rotting, and she felt weak and cowardly. She felt deeply sorry for An, so she only knew how to offer gifts, fruit cakes, and little material items, even though she knew she couldn't make up for those broken wounds.

***

X Cinema, December 2012.

"Do you recall the first movie we saw together?"

"Superman vs. Batman?" That night, we went to a pub together, and the next morning, we both went to the movies."

"At that moment, I was asked if I had been fatigued, and I replied that I hadn't felt anything!"

"Then you must take advantage. I only have a few days in Saigon, so I won't constantly be able to be with you!"

Phuong grinned as she looked at the man "in the flesh" in front of her. Following the film, the two shared fries. Mac was always faultless in front of her, with the same way of talking and amazing harmony.

But it had already been 5 years; wake up, Phuong! She could hear the admonition in her thoughts.

"I used to think Saigon was a lovely place. Full of possibilities, full of freedom. But, after a long day at work, I and Ly can't even see each other's faces every day."

"I warned you not to marry so young!" Phuong's tone was half-joking, half-serious. *"Isn't it better to just be friends, go out occasionally, and then go home separately?"*

"Haha! But, you know, not everything you wish can be accomplished?" Mac cut Phuong off. *"How about you? Why do you continue without pausing? if you don't cherish a girl's youth; there will be a day of sorrow."*

"I gave you my entire youth, but you refuse to take it?"

The talk abruptly came to a halt. His aroma, his passionate hug, his first soft kiss... She couldn't forget those first few seconds. She had been trying for a long time to break him of her addiction, but it was surprisingly tough. What did you have that other men didn't? Why did he make her so unhappy? Why was he there? He came to her at the age of 22, just as all faith in her was fading. He learned to recognize the chasm, loneliness, and schism in her soul. It was fate that she was delighted and angry at the same moment.

Mac emerged when Phuong had everything: the brilliant beauty of her twenties, the job advancement, the soul that loved life returning after many events, Phuong remembered. Still, something inside of her made her feel as if she was looking for this love relationship to cover up her deepest sorrows, anxieties, and inadequacies.

Phuong realized she was correct when she wasn't too content with what she had. That love evaporated just as she thought and mustered the courage to reveal her feelings to him. He refused; his girlfriend had been there for a long time; did she know what to do with the pain? She had realized since then that life was not as simple as she had imagined. At the time, Phuong allowed work consume the majority of her time, but she concentrated on it and converted it into motivation to help her overcome the loss.

Phuong wore more makeup than she had done before. Sharp lines drew attention to her eyes, and her lips were painted with a deep crimson lipstick. How many times did Phuong swallow back tears, just to realize that she could still face everything on her own? How could someone like her succumb to and let the passion of love wash away in such a way?

Phuong burst out laughing. *"So, when you're in love, don't blame people for being disloyal to you; instead, blame yourself for not looking closely enough"*.

***

After the movie, Phuong said her goodbyes to Mac. The room was dark when she got home. Phuong opened the cupboard and reached for a bottle of cold water, thinking to herself that An could enjoy his first days outside the four prison walls. An's hobbies of bar club, shisha, music, and beauty would definitely make his life better now, allowing him to forget the bitterness of the past.

From the day An moved in with Phuong till now, the two have rarely met and spoken. It was tough for them both to face each other normally as before. An was still sleeping when Phuong awoke to go to work. When Phuong was getting ready to go to night, she left the door and lights open so An could enter without having to ring the doorbell. Whether he was awake or not, Phuong could constantly smell alcohol on An's body.

Phuong always had a glimmer of optimism in her heart. She convinced herself that the past was like collected bruises; if you didn't touch it, the agony would gradually fade away. And who knew that as time passed, everything would revert to its previous state, just as An and Phuong had predicted in their hearts.

Phuong silently submerged herself in the sound of the shower in the bathtub, then softly dried her hair and examined herself in the mirror for a long time. It had been 5 years since she went out of the house without her face covered in thick powder, because she never felt secure showing her bare face.

Phuong became aware of a mole on her face behind her eyes unconsciously. How could that be? Phuong became terrified when the picture of the baby's face resurfaced in the mirror.

Phuong yelled. Her eyes pricked. She sat down on the ground, her shoulders trembling now and then.

Phuong felt relaxed again after quickly peeling off the shell and inhaling a bit more medical marijuana. *"It was all a trick of the light... Because I was exhausted..."*

Phuong succumbed to the strength of accumulated fatigue. Thoughts raced through her mind at breakneck speed. Her weekend was now more complete with Mac by her side. Mac wished to reconnect with her. Mac loved her and was no longer ashamed of it. However, Phuong was still tortured because Mac had a wife, and she did not want to deprive other people of their happiness. She had no idea what would happen if she was burdened with this relationship that had no future.

Before lying down on the bed, Phuong put a layer of cream on her face and lip balm. She was startled when the doorbell rang. An never rang the doorbell when he came home because this house was no longer fresh to him. Despite the fact that she had no idea who the visitor was, she jumped out of bed and carelessly opened the door.

The door swung open. The heavy odor of alcohol invaded her, making her uneasy. She recognized it was the blue checkered shirt Mac had just donned in an unexpected moment. Mac hugged her so firmly that she almost fell to the ground. Her lips found his instinctively, and the two immersed themselves in a kiss that had never been so passionate, never so powerful.

Phuong had been waiting for this moment for 5 years, but he did not expect it to come true. Both were enamored with longing, but when their bodies covered one other and sweat saturated their bodies, Phuong understood this was no longer a dream.

The two stared up at the ceiling after the pleasure had worn off. The sound of the rotating fan shattered the night's silence:

"What brought you to see me?"

"I can't forget about you."

"I previously stated that I would not be able to accomplish it for you and return to Saigon to work for a young graduate's pay!"

"Because, well, I'm a jerk. I don't have the courage to go through that again."

"So you deserted me? Just because I have nothing but love to bind you to?"

Mac's silence made Phuong burst out laughing. She turned to avoid Mac's stare. Love, no matter how much it was cherished, was never forever.

Phuong wondered why she always acted in such a "noble" manner. Perhaps they forgive past mistakes because they adored someone who gave them everything.

People who were in love could talk gibberish and do dumb things.

"All I want to do right now is slap you!"

"OK, then you'll do it! I can't even bring you something good!"

"So, what brought you to me today?"

"Because I need you. And one hell of a thing was making its way to every corner of Saigon, and I will always remember you."

"What if you don't need me any longer?"

Phuong turned to face Mac, who was fast asleep. Despite his peaceful demeanor, Mac does not exude a delicate and tender affection. He used to be a strong passion that drove her insane. Phuong's palm stroked each line on Mac's face: the creases on the brow, the eyes, the bridge of the nose, and the soft lips that made her "drunk" the first time she saw them. However, it was also the first time she had seen him up close. *"And how come it was so close yet so far away?"*

The unidentified relationship between her and Mac, unsure whether to call it quit.

Phuong hadn't been able to sleep next to anyone in a long time. There was also peace and fulfillment of desire. She had more conflicting feelings than anyone else. She was thinking about guilt for some reason. Then, in her dream, she found herself lost in the campus of a magnificent white villa, laying alone among willow trees. The slowly drooping leaves caressed her skin.

The wooden door to the villa appears to be unlocked. Phuong reflected to herself. She dared to open the door and slog up the stairs. The door was locked as soon as she walked in. The sound of the piano reverberating from nowhere startled her. Following in her footsteps, the light in the room turned on.

Phuong walked into a room that was completely white. The boy with a white sweater and blue sweatpants stood at the window, waiting for her. The boy smiled, his hands moving the Yoyo softly. The Yoyo unknowingly fell into the garden. The youngster burst into tears. She extended her hand to wait for the boy to grasp her hand, and the boy extended his hand to take it, but the farther they were from each other, the harder they tried.

"Mommy! Don't abandon me, Mom! I adore you so much! I know I'm mistaken! It's freezing in here, Mom!"

Phuong awoke. She trembled in her thin shirt, tears welling up in her eyes, plagued by a severe migraine. She longed for her son. That year's memories seemed to sneak into her every thought. They never let go of her. They clung to her, not letting her breathe for even a second.

She then laid down on the bed and promptly fell asleep again. Mac awoke unexpectedly a few minutes later. He gave Phuong a meaningful glance. He was perplexed by her concern and the tears that remained in the corners of her eyes. He softly touched her shoulder to console her, despite the fact that she didn't hear or speak to him.

Chapter 4

"Seeing someone always behaving 'fine' leads others to believe they no longer need to pay attention to them. Humans are typically so!"

***

07/02/2002

The Pullman Hotel

9.30 PM

Phuong closed her eyes and sat calmly for her sister to make up her makeup. She had never imagined that she could be covered in such expensive foundation and have her lips painted with such expensive lipsticks.

She learned today that Mr. Huy Khiem had a party at this Pullman hotel to summarize the company's major activities. This was a gathering where she could meet famous artists, screenwriters, and entertainment management "bosses."

Phuong came here as a distant relative of Mr. Huy Khiem for the first time to attend such a large occasion. She had been puzzled and bewildered for a month, unable to establish her position in this relationship or what function she played at this period.

Mr. Khiem didn't call her very much. Sometimes she just went out to dinner with him and listened to him talk about the pressures of being a producer, and other times she walked with him all afternoon without saying anything. He frequently gave money for each occasion by placing envelopes in her bag while she wasn't looking.

Looking at the money in his hand, Phuong agreed to a condition not to sleep with him. And Phuong thought that was unusual. This interaction was more "nice" and strange than she had anticipated. Was it possible that he had affections for her and respected her?

She would sooner starve to death than sleep with a 40-year-old man her father's age.

Phuong was not interested in show business on that particular day. Her daily schedule was meticulously planned in order to maximize her earnings. Every day, she worked part-time, read books, and watched online docs. Phuong did not comprehend at the time that the flavor of people was more essential than the smell of money. She also had no idea that gambling with money was riskier than she assumed. But, deep down, she believed that money was the most powerful eraser in the world, regardless of whether memories or records were erased. She hoped that her bleak background would soon change as well.

Phuong approached the celebration with the most confident air, having just done her cosmetics and changed into a stunning white gown. But she only saw odd faces wherever she went. Loneliness washed through Phuong like a black mirror.

Phuong sat on a high chair at the celebration bar, her dress split displaying her long white legs. She was the only one sitting. She sipped her bitter wine while listening to the calm Acoustic music. That was also the period when she felt the most at ease and aware. Her ears were selective, pushing back laughter, the voice of dialogue concealed in the echoing sound of the guitar. She'd heard that playing the guitar was the greatest way to avoid distractions. Wouldn't her hands be happier if she was playing the guitar or writing?

Phuong didn't know why she was alive, but she knew she had to force herself to stay awake from now on. The critics would vanish in an instant. Why should she care about people's tongues if she didn't trade herself to achieve what she wanted?

After stating the party's cause, the dignified man on the podium looked down at Phuong, his eyes filled with indescribable emotions. Phuong was too unskilled at the time to recognize the hidden dangers. Her mind was racing and she couldn't sit up straight.

Phuong had just gotten out of her chair when she passed out. She was surrounded by a pitch-black night. Just a monotonous black tone, but Phuong had no idea it was that dreadful color that was causing terrible cuts in her life that were difficult to heal.

***

**In December of 2012,
District 2's X Center**

Phuong drank the last of the coke at the X Center restaurant. Outside the window, white rain fell, as if threatening to bury her here forever.

She was alone at 11 a.m. in this cool restaurant with soft music, but it was so frightening. It was music that suited her mental state while also creating a deep sense of discomfort.

Months of executing a media campaign for a new project always wind up being tedious and time-consuming. Three days had passed since Phuong and Mac had spent the night together. It turned out that sleeping with a man she once loved was not as wonderful as she had imagined. It was only skin-to-skin, lips-to-lip, and then that was it.

Phuong exited the business after picking up the phone to talk with a colleague. A pang of shame welled up inside her as she walked in the rain. When she was in a terrible mood, just glancing at something mundane would make her entire spirit sink.

Previously, Phuong only differentiated between two concepts: "love" and "not love," and she refused to accept any explanation when her sentiments were not reciprocated, including the one given by Mac. She never imagined he'd appreciate that feeling five years ago, because he didn't select her.

Now that she had come to accept it, where was the evidence that Mac wished to return? He was supposed to be considering his family, wasn't he? What if she had arrived first and met Mac earlier? Wouldn't that be ideal? He eventually broke all ties to her and the rest of his former life. Had he earned her undying love, or ought she to have given up?

As she made her way down the lane to her house, Phuong looked at the moon. Few people knew about her sensitive side once the sun went down, though the world seen her slog through the day.

Phuong was shocked to realize that something seemed to be following her shadow in the moonlight as her mind meandered along a line of thought. As she lowered her pace, the thing stopped moving faster. Faster she ran, the more it pursued. She ran to the end of the alley, where she crouchingly waited for a time, her heart pounding.

Phuong stuck her head out as she heard footsteps approaching. The thing transformed into a towering humanoid when the light from the street lighting shone in, revealing soulless eyes. She couldn't see his face since he was holding a sharp knife. Something horrible had transpired, according to her intuition. Despite the fact that her thoughts was no longer clear, she attempted to approach the odd man calmly:

"What exactly do you want?"

"You must ask yourself what went wrong!"

"I'm not doing anything wrong here. I know how I live!"

"Are you certain? Is it because you enjoy hurting other people's family happiness? Your face has to be a little uglier for you to quit doing this, right?"

The man approached Phuong quickly, holding a sharp blade in his hand. Another unknown man soon ran over, giving the tattooed hand a hook kick to the ribs, while her heart was at its most frail, and her mind was at its most scared. She was taken aback by the man in front of her. *"Why did the rude guy I met in the elevator the other day appear here?"*

The two men battled for a time before collapsing on the road. On avoid hurting the man and defend himself, Phuong swiftly picked up the knife that had just fallen to the ground and held it out in front of him, as if threatening to hurt him at any time:

"Who forced you to do this?" Isn't it also your pastime to ruin people's lives?"

"Sleeping with a married individual and continuing to act as if nothing happened?" Women can now think for themselves."

For a few seconds, Phuong's thoughts wandered. Taking advantage of the momentum, the tattooed hand seized her foot and kicked the knife she was carrying onto the ground, forcing her hand to bleed, before fleeing. Unbeknownst to her, the man she met in the elevator the other day ran to help Phuong up. Phuong giggled, as if not afraid, murmuring Mac's name to herself. *"So, I just had a 'jealous attack,' right?"*

"I saw you again!" Because he was preoccupied with Phuong's thoughts, Khanh spoke first.

"Thank you for helping me". Phuong was perplexed. *"I'm at a loss for words when I see you in this scenario."*

"It's okay; you've simply been unlucky. Would you like a drink to relax?"

"...." Phuong remained silent for a minute, unsure what to do.

"Take it as my restitution for my error the other day, and consider it your restitution to me this time." Okay?"

Phuong gazed up at the man standing in front of her, puzzled by the incident that occurred so rapidly, quietly thanking him for appearing at the right time.

***

Khanh and Phuong sipped their beers. Because it being a workday, the two sat in a BBQ restaurant that served 24 hours a day. Khanh initiated a dialogue after observing Phuong's hesitation and avoidance of his gaze:

"Don't go home so late the next time. After all, you are a lady."

"Thank you so much. I'll learn from my mistakes. Oh, this bar has fantastic appetizers and alcohol."

Khanh grinned as Phuong introduced himself. He fixed his gaze on her unconsciously.

"It's not that I'm a chatterbox... But I just overheard it... "Do you have a boyfriend who is married?"

"I didn't intend to." Phuong exhaled a sigh. "The only problem is that it is right now. He used to make me happy. He refused to confess it. I can't get out now that he wants to come back to me despite having a family..."

"..."

"He is someone who has introduced me to many interesting topics." When I was doubting everything, he supported me..."

"But it's only a recollection... Do you believe it's worth it for the time being? What's up now that his lady has spotted you?"

"I'm not certain. Now all I want is to be free."

After consuming a bottle of wine in one sitting, Phuong turned to Khanh and asked, "Do you want to continue arguing this topic?"

"But, Mr. Khanh, what are you doing in the building where I work?"

"Ah... I am the Director of a studio on the 9th floor, and I direct a few film projects if you are interested. What about you?"

"I work in the media business. I guess I've met you somewhere before; you appear familiar to me."

"Did you ever "swipe right" on Tinder for me?"

Phuong was taken aback. It appeared that she and this man had a predestined relationship. Furthermore, she knew from conversing with Khanh that he was looking for a few new scripts to make into movies, which was the item she was most excited to meet.

She had a passion for writing for a long time. She already had dozens of scripts buried in her PC. She had, however, yet to find the perfect timing and investors. Many people had objected to making a film based on her script. She was claimed to be unexceptional, to lack traits, and to be without a connection, therefore she ended there. Phuong herself refused to be satisfied; she desired more.

Khanh was the first person she knew who worked in the film industry as a director or producer. He spoke passionately about the films he had done, the stress he had experienced, and the marvels of art he had witnessed while traversing the world. One could see the energy in his eyes.

Noticing Khanh's interest, Phuong proceeded to talk about her dream of writing and the script she was working on, hoping that he would pay attention. She didn't expect much, and she merely tried to approach him. Not to add that, because the relationship was considered a "passport" in the country where she lived, this was one of her ruses for attracting the new "investor," who was him. Build a nice relationship with Khanh, and things would be much easier for her.

She would soon become well-known. She would soon become the powerful person she had always desired.

"However, how could I capture a stranger's interest from the first moment we met? Furthermore, the individual with whom I wished to work for

a long time and made my job easier?

Instant Love - This is the solution".

***

December 2012

Ly warmed up the rice cooker and carefully laid each dish on the table. She checked her phone every now and then to see if Mac was ready to go home at this time. She examined herself in the mirror, her short curly hair perfectly combed, her pink lips tinged with lipstick. She was content with her natural beauty.

Ly sighed; she hadn't had time to cook for her husband or pamper herself in a long time. She then rested her hand on her stomach once more. Since Mac's return to Vietnam, she had been pregnant for two months. Ly never imagined she would be able to live such a great life for her family, her husband, and her children.

Despite the fact that she lacked the attractiveness of "thousands of individuals," Ly understood how to apply makeup and draw attention to her specialty.

Ly and Mac's one-month wedding anniversary was today. They've known each other for seven or eight years, but the number of times they had gotten angry, broken up, and reconnected was uncountable. Ly used to live as if she were an animal, not a human. When she was five years old, her parents divorced. Soon after, her father was arrested for causing a tragic traffic accident and then fleeing. Ly's mother raised four brothers by herself until she was an adult.

Ly recalled being frequently insulted about her family by acquaintances in high school. Ly had not expected her pain to manifest in this manner. For more than 20 years, she had been a girl with an expressionless face.

She was still upset and indignant at first, but the hurt gradually faded over time. Lying about missing school. She was getting tattoos all over her body, including her arms, neck, and chest. Ly was hooked to tattoos; she used to be terrified and in pain while tattooing, but she became attracted to the sensation of each little needle imprinted on her flesh.

Then Ly got a job as a bartender. She had no formal education, was unable to sing, and was unable to act in films. To continue on this route, she only needed a gift for bartending, a little beauty, and long legs.

But that was not enough to sustain life. There were numerous paths to success in life. At the time, she chose to date a wealthy young man. She didn't care about that brat two years her junior; she cared more about his money. She ran into Mac again when she was fed up with her love-money life.

Initially, the two were merely impressed by each other's appearance and did not fall in love like lightning. Mac was a prestigious university in Marketing in England and was on summer vacation in Vietnam, where they first met at a pub 7 years ago. For such a short period, Mac only wanted to know her in the form of "love-not-binding".

However, after numerous coffee dates, watching movies, and passionate "love" in bed, both Ly and Mac found themselves missing each other when they couldn't see each other every week, and feeling unhappy if they didn't accept each other communications received from the other person. They decided to declare their love for each other, then simply hold each other's hearts. In the end, both Ly and Mac chose to be together in this way.

However, neither Ly's nor Mac's family members approved of the marriage. Ly, a female with head-to-toe tattoos and a bartending profession, was not accepted by Mac's family. Ly's family had a history of criminal activity. Neither party felt the relationship can go this far.

Ly and Mac agreed to separate for a while since they were both depressed and fatigued. Mac went on to pursue a master's degree in marketing in the United Kingdom. Then, 5 years later, 3 months ago, in a drunken meeting at a pub, he and Ly couldn't keep it together. Despite the family's concerns, Mac was obliged to marry Ly, relocate to Saigon, and start afresh.

Ly was startled by the creaking sound of the door opening. All previous ideas have been broken. This was Mac. He gave her a friendly smile. He kissed her forehead as usual and then softly entered the room:

"Did you eat dinner?"

"So you'll have to eat by yourself. I'm exhausted today and simply want to sleep."

"Do you know what day it is today?" Ly began to express her dissatisfaction.

"I'm not the man I was when we first fell in love, Honey." Mac exclaimed loudly. "Please don't make me guess what you're thinking."

Ly gave Mac a scowl. She abruptly flipped the bag upside down on the table. There were pictures of Mac and a strange female all over the place. Mac was taken aback; wasn't that the period of Mac and Phuong's meeting?

"Are you following to me? Do you not believe me?"

"Did you give any hints for me to believe you?" What do you do for a living, who do you hang out with, are there evenings when you don't come home and don't answer the phone? Do you know any husband and wife who are as apathetic as we are?"

" … "

"Honestly, did you tell me to come to Saigon to live with you because you can't forget that girl, not because you love me?"

Ly's voice didn't tremble as tears streamed down her cheeks. Mac gazed at Ly, his face filled with tiredness and sadness. He wasn't awake enough to say anything to Ly at this moment. Despite Ly's queries echoing endlessly in his ears, he discreetly moved his feet on the stairs leading up to the chamber.

Ly glanced blankly at the plate of rice that had been sitting on the table for a long time. The couple's one-month wedding anniversary turned out to be a disaster. The phone abruptly rang, interrupting the silence.

"In this case, Ly, I failed. While I was on the move, she had someone assist her." The voice of a strange man burst out - he was also the only close bartender at the former tavern she worked at.

Ly chuckled, since this was a love story, and only women could solve it together.

***

10.00 PM

S Department, District 2

My name was Xuan An, and I was 27 years old this year. My life was not as tranquil as the name my grandma gave me, no matter how much I yearn for happiness and stability. It was, indeed, my grandmother, not my parents.

After a long day working as a mechanic at the workshop, I washed and rapidly dried my short hair. My supervisor abruptly let me go on the final day of the month, but he only paid me half of what I deserved. Obviously, I wasn't rude, yet all I got in return was derision. It was difficult for someone with a criminal record, such as myself, to restart their lives. Accepting me as an employee was challenging; deciding to pay me a living wage was also difficult.

If you couldn't alter the situation, why not change your attitude? Was this world ever as simple as it appeared? Get rid of that nonsense theory. What else could I do now that life had trapped me? Confrontation or compromise? After all, I couldn't seem to find the joy in life that I did before entering those four walls.

Swallowing the cold rice Phuong had cooked on the table, I felt both glad and unhappy about the money I had earned in the month since I had been released from prison. Going to prison was not as frightening as I had imagined; it was just that living behind bars made me forget what it was like to be human. I was still trying to remain calm, to smile, to face things calmly. My faith, on the other hand, had long since faded.

I remembered the days of adversity and suffering in Quang Nam. I had lived with my grandmother since I was a child, so I was unfamiliar with my parents' looks. My gender was not the same as everyone else's, despite the word "Female" on my birth certificate. Because, despite being approached by male friends from childhood, I preferred to gaze at females' lovely lips and naked shoulders, and I was captivated with those wonderful curves. I had resolved to live with the appearance of a boy since I was 12 years old. I ditched skirts in favor of shorts and t-shirts, and I chopped my hair short in order to feel happier and more confident.

But it was also what made me lonely.

I understood that not everyone was born with someone by their side. It was not surprising that some people were always lonely. I was merely one of them. No one wanted to be near an uncommon person like myself back then. Although no one knows what the term "normal" means here.

And Phuong appeared in my life like a flash of light.

When I first saw Phuong smile at me in high school, it felt like a whole new universe had opened up to me. The concord between our families and personalities was predetermined fate.

When my peers teased me about my gender when they put my name on the board during recess in class or in online communities back then, just hearing Phuong's voice murmur in my ear gave me more motivation to overcome.

I recalled how I used to look forward to Phuong's text messages every night, becoming anxious when she didn't respond. I recalled riding our bikes in the rain, when our shirts were soaked, when Phuong's goodnight words were whispered in our ears, and when we both shivered while eating ice cream by the roadside.

But all that happened between us was now a distant memory.

I was 17 years old when Phuong chose to leave Quang Nam and move to Saigon to start a new life. But, only a few weeks later, I arrived in this lovely city to work because my grandmother could no longer afford to pay for my schooling. I tried to make ends meet by working odd jobs like waitressing and selling and sending money to her every month.

Furthermore, I wanted to defend the person I loved with all my might, even if I couldn't always protect myself.

That life behind bars, those were remarkable recollections for me. Although I tried to listen to the "seniors" earlier, there were occasions when I was beaten as if I were about to repent just because they didn't like my expressionless face, didn't like the "pleasant" thing. My peculiarity. There were moments when I adopted the role of both a physical and symbolic "servant": I prepared water and acted as a "comfort lady" for some other long-term gay inmates, all in order to maintain my humble life. I wasn't protesting, conforming, or being sectarian with anyone. People continued to call me a "lovely" criminal, but I had no idea how long that generosity would remain.

At the time, I wished I could just take a nap and wake up to discover that I was nothing.

During my months in prison, I wrote to Phuong every day, only to discover that there was still hope. I knew Phuong had been active and was steadily making her way to the top on her own road, so in the months that followed in the re-education camp, I also became a busy person in my own way. I learnt how to cut my own hair, sew, plant trees, visit the library, and study law and policy. I was confident that my efforts would make her pleased. I believed that love could be conveyed from one soul to another, even if the loved one had died.

If it hadn't been for me, there would have been someone else to take care of Phuong, someone ten thousand times better. I knew there were various ways to love and that it didn't have to be forced. It was like attempting to put on a great shirt but not being able to get it under your wrist. If it was, it would likewise break, have holes, and would not last long.

Chapter 5

"Unhappy people, like myself, frequently cling to the past, dwell in the memories, and lament the things they missed."

***

Phuong listened to the song's final sentence. She always set aside some time after work to write, to finish unfinished screenplays.

For a long time, Phuong felt distinct from the rest of the world, possibly when she reached 17 years old. She didn't dislike her family or friends; she just felt humiliated by poverty.

Who was to say that life on a higher plane didn't taste more enticing?

To escape the mediocrity that life had bestowed upon Phuong, she had expended all of her energy studying and trading things she had never considered. She used to work 16 hours a day, with no friends or frivolous play, to forget about the problems of the past. She didn't chose someone to be by her side because she believed it would be better to be alone and that love would sap her power. Wasn't it simpler when you lived selfishly?

Even if there was no response, Phuong grasped and energetically decided on work. Love, on the other hand, may abandon her at any time, even on a wonderful day that Phuong had not wished for.

In Saigon, where it was stated that success was determined by each individual, Phuong thought she was not in the correct position. She desired more.

Looking around the workplace, only Ha - her assistant - worked hard to complete each task. Phuong grinned, harshly, because she wanted Ha to mature, to understand that work did not happen by chance, and success did not fall from the sky. It was impossible not to work hard and pay the price for what you desired.

Maybe Ha had no affections for her, maybe Ha thought she was no different from a "dark boss" at work, but on that day, no one "spreaded roses" so that Phuong might have such a position. now. After all, Phuong merely wanted to be recognized, to know that she was valued in the eyes of others.

Looking at the mountain of paperwork that needed to be paid and the reports that needed to be delivered by tonight, Ha sighed and wished she could dig a hole and hide herself. It had been four or five months in a gorgeous nook, but all she had been doing was creating contracts, payment forms, ordering meals for everyone in the room, and then delivering all day.

"Running errands can be very profitable at times!" Ha reflected to herself.

Phuong was silently observed by Ha. Ha had never seen Phuong smile that brightly. Phuong's effort, exhaustion, and boredom were hidden under that flawless exterior. Ha, on the other hand, admired her young employer greatly. She realized Phuong had a lot to teach her. She always knew how to regulate her words and self-image, always smiled quietly and solved one problem at a time, and treated others the way she did. In a nutshell, Phuong's bravery should not be underestimated.

However, in this universe, there was no such thing as a "blue fairy" or someone with a noble soul who could tolerate everything. Ha was aware that Phuong was still hiding her tension and worry behind her daily routine. But that was the way the game of life worked. Right now, the world was too cruel and deadly for dreamers. How could she have survived if she wasn't soulless, shameless, cunning, or cruel? Was there another option?

Ha checked her watch; it was already 9 p.m. She hurriedly packed her belongings and prepared to depart. But, in fact, no one was waiting for her anymore? Her parents went to bed early, and her boyfriend became bored because she didn't spend enough time with him. It was probably simply some cold rice and fish dishes waiting for her at home now.

"It's all right! It's better than nothing late at night".

Ha was going to "run away" as she slipped across the door of the boss's chamber, when she heard Phuong's familiar voice echo back:

"Are you on your way home now?" "Are you working so late?"

Ha was taken aback by Phuong's question. Phuong unintentionally invited Ha to a late-night meal. Ha couldn't keep her surprise from showing. Both were feeling empty and lonely right now, and they needed to share, even if it was simply sitting next to each other and listening to each other's exhaustion through sighs.

10 pm. McDonald's had been limited. Only Ha and Phuong were left with a few bits of salad and chicken, as well as the unfinished Coke.

"At first, I believed you despised me. Give me a lot of work, then make me correct it over and over. Who would have guessed that there would come a day when we would all go out to supper together?"

"So you believe I'm good to you now?"

"At the very least, you give me my time and encouragement! I want to learn more about you, what you enjoy and what you desire, so that I can do well on your work."

"Be cautious; knowing too much about me is not a good thing. Don't cause yourself any harm."

Phuong smiled as she watched the young girl begin to relate anecdotes about her life. Ha lived a fairly extravagant life, obsessed with emotions and passion. When Ha recounted about short, transitory love stories, Phuong recognized the fervor of her twenties in those eyes, understood the shyness combined with anger, and felt sadness when she told about the times. When traveling from Da Lat to Saigon, she was duped and her latent passion went unsatisfied.

"Do you genuinely enjoy your job?" Phuong continued to question Ha.

"It's all right, sister. I'll let you in on a little secret: my true love is singing... But doesn't that sound a little far-fetched?"

"I'm young and free to do whatever I want. You must understand what you are working for and what you require to obtain what you desire."

"You know, sometimes I wonder why I'm alive... After working for the company for a while, I'm not sure what I have left. I don't have a close friend that understands me, despite having a large number of social pals, my boyfriend doesn't relate, and my parents have no idea what the hell I'm doing..."

"..."

"Ah, it doesn't really matter, but I think about him when I dine with you." He and you are both really peaceful, which is something I haven't been able to achieve."

"Who?"

"My ex... lover. It's quite difficult for me to love anyone. Previously, anybody who came to me did so not only for my beauty, but also to obtain something from me. They come when they need it and go when they don't. However, when I met him, all my reservations vanished. Have you ever known someone who always offers you optimism for the future and never asks you for anything?"

Phuong laughed and nodded slightly in agreement. Ha was intrigued by Phuong's demeanor and wanted to understand more about her "idol's" life. Did anyone realize that when we came close to a star, we would notice that it was also rough and thorny, not as bright as when we looked at it from afar?

Looking through the glass pane at McDonald's, Phuong had the unexpected realization that her heart towards An was not one of love, but one of compassion. An was the one who taught her that learning to love someone was far superior to learning to hate them. She had the opportunity to go to different places and meet new people because to An. Because of An, she believed she was capable of achieving her goals. Understanding An, on the other hand, was too difficult for her. She couldn't reply adequately to An's affection for her. Phuong did not let anyone hurt her, yet she did not stop tormenting herself after that night.

Phuong used to have a vacant face and the generosity that came with being a professional workaholic. She thought she'd beaten everything, so she didn't need a guy at her side, just a genuine friend like An.

During her stay in prison, An suffered alone; nasty things were dealt with just by her. No one encouraged her, no one understood her thoughts, and she didn't have time to explain. She was powerless over herself. When she thought of An, she realized she couldn't compensate for what An had gone through. *"Who is deserving of his adoration?"*

"Is it human nature to be lonely all the time, even if we are occasionally blessed with the affection of others?"

Until now, even when everything appeared to be going well, Phuong felt unable to grasp, to discover the entire trust inherent in a relationship like any other regular individual because Phuong was aware that she was not an ordinary person, and her heart, in a way, had long since withered trust.

Phuong's life was not random, but rather planned.

***

December 2012

Ha returned to the small tight room she and her lover had purchased from a neighbor one Sunday morning. Paintings and colored bottles scattered throughout the room made her breathing more difficult. Quick, she hadn't lived with him in about two years.

He was Minh Nhat, the sun that shone brightly in her life. That ray of light, however, now belonged to someone else.

He hadn't been here in a week. He had left her thinking he was on a business trip. Once upon a time, Ha happened to meet Nhat in a cafe near her home where she worked part-time. He frequented that tavern for creative inspiration. Ha was smitten by Nhat's drawings, which made her determined to pursue him. After a year of dating, the two decided to move into a cohabiting house to see what would happen if it was true love.

Why strive to love but not truly love? With Ha, she believed that even if individuals had been honest with you, you should not believe that you understood them. There were still dark areas, flaws in them that the other side had never told us about. To some extent, there were people who always wanted for what they didn't have, even to the point of trading their happiness for fleeting items that were more pleasant than the present. That was why marriage was becoming increasingly hurried, arriving swiftly and departing without attachment.

Nhat was a fine artist who enjoyed drawing, but he understood that enthusiasm could not sustain him. He, on the other hand, was obsessed with painting. To be fair, he was a gifted and adaptive individual. If life was imposed upon him, he could still work as an office designer, occasionally performed at Acoustic pubs, and started a restaurant with his father's sponsorship money.

But, most significantly, he was uninterested in them. He wished to be in charge of his own life. After graduating from university, he chose to work as a salesman at Ministop during the day in order to get experience and have more time in the evening to make images. Despite the fact that he had no significant outcomes, he gave himself a false sense of satisfaction when he mistakenly believed that one day he would meet his time.

Last Sunday, at this time, Ha walked home with a cup of black coffee in her hand. When she was in a terrible mood, she would reward herself with a cup of strong black coffee, sipping a touch of bitterness and feeling her heart find some calm after the salty days.

She sat down on the bed without even a grin, the smell of paint in his palms making her feel bored:

"Don't work like hell without a burning desire, okay? When I look at you fatigued, I don't know what to say..." Nhat drew and shifted his gaze to her.

"Is there any career that may provide me with a pleasant existence without requiring me to work hard?" Ha had a thought.

"Why don't you look for a job that pays a little less but makes you feel more at ease?" Minh Nhat continued to provide advice.

"Then look in the mirror, honey. Painting is your dream. You lived sloppily every day and couldn't generate any money off of it, forcing you to work as a menial employee at Ministop." Ha objected, unable to suppress her anguish.

"..." Minh Nhat kept silent.

"You can't even safeguard your dream, so why urge me to stop?"

"Of course, I'm not qualified to say that. I can't promise you anything..." Minh Nhat's voice softened. "... Or we... stop here... You and I do not have the same objectives. I'm afraid I can't help you either..."

Ha's eyes were welling up. Every time she reflected on the past, she felt as if a weight was being placed on her shoulder.

Minh Nhat had never returned to Ha's place since that day. According to the family's plan, he chose to operate a coffee business. The dream of becoming a famous painter was also just kept in the back of his mind.

"When I entered your realm, I used all of my strength."
I just hope you respect me a bit, share a little with me,...
Then maybe our narrative won't end there..."

Ha read the final line she scribbled in her diary. If he hadn't given up on that day so readily, things could have turned out differently. She pondered what her past had bestowed upon her. Was that the maturation she needed to live a better life?

Now, Ha was too lazy to battle every day for something she didn't really believe in, was not passionate about, and didn't want to spend time on.

Ha surfed Facebook. She saw Minh Nhat's post. He was swiftly engaged to a girl with a well-known face on the street. She couldn't tell whether it was a joke or a play...

Minh Nhat was a sweet dream for Ha. Minh Nhat means "The Sun" in Vietnamese. The moon was always superior to the sun. Knowing that people were only real to themselves when the moon was dark, but the sun was the life they had to fight every day. Minh Nhat forced her to be content with what she had.

But Ha didn't want to live that way. She still desired to be free to dream in her world; she desired to be like someone, such as her boss; she desired to have something to pursue, whether it was an unrealistic passion for singing or the knowledge required to open a cafe...

Ha realized that in order to have one thing, she had to give up something other, which was the concept of "opportunity cost."

***

Lush Bar, Sai Gon

10.00 PM
Phuong, engrossed in the music of the bar, stared at her face in a glass of wine. She hadn't gone to such packed and bustling areas in a long time.

Phuong had heard that unhappy people, like her, often clung to the past, lived in memories, and lamented the things they had missed.

She desired to end her terrible life. In the end, the previous separation triumphed over her and Mac's tight, informal link of attachment. Her mind, on the other hand, couldn't stop thinking about the pleasant times she spent with him.

Phuong sipped on a tumbler of wine. Her vision became hazy. She only wanted Mac to remember one thing: That there was someone who truly and unreservedly loved him.

She was inebriated when she felt a hand on her waist. From behind, a certain man was tormenting her body. She tried to aggressively release go of his hand, but he refused to let go any farther.

Phuong was startled by a "pop" sound from behind him. She returned her gaze. Who's in the chained denim shirt, coping with the curly-haired guy who just touched her?

It was Khanh once more. He always appeared in front of her when she was in the most danger.

She and Khanh walked to the bar's VIP section for additional solitude. She couldn't figure out why she and Khanh had so much to talk about despite the fact that they rarely communicated.

"You saved me yet again." When the booze had taken effect in her body, Phuong laughed and drewled.

"You can return the favor by inviting me to this wine." Khanh sipped his drink. "How far have you gotten with the screenplay?"

"I, too, am writing. Because I am new at writing, I still have many flaws. In addition, I'm "stuck" in too many places.

"As long as you persevere, everything is alright." Khanh lit a cigarette, took a deep breath, and resumed speaking. "I'm not very good at anything, but it's only because I'm persistent and don't give up easily that I've gotten to where I am now."

***

23.00 PM. 07/02/2002

Residence, District 7

Phuong awoke startled as she heard music playing in the room's corner. Phuong's head was foggy from drinking, and she had no memory of having had so much alcohol. The cocktail appeared to have some sort of medication in it.

In a drab, gray room with yellow lights, Phuong was by herself. Her gaze flitted all over the space. Photos of Huy Khiem's family, accolades, and book shelves abound, but the stars seemed so chilly.

Phuong experienced some unease. An's number was called, but he didn't pick up. Once... twice... No response either.

Phuong pretended to close her eyes when she heard a sigh outside the door and heard approaching footsteps. Who else could it be but the man who brought her here, smelling that familiar perfume? Phuong shuddered. His rapacious hands started to prowl about her body. She was aware that it couldn't continue. She pushed the man away with all her might, but he grabbed her and slapped her painfully.

She started crying because she didn't want to risk her life in the hands of a man who was that much older than her. He tore her scanty skirt and raked her neck with his hands for a considerable amount of time, like a ravenous wolf. The scratches were becoming more and more severe. Phuong accidentally struck him in the head with the bag that was on the table. Despite his cry, the man held onto her tightly. He was lying on top of her, piercing her violently to the core, where unceasing blood gushed.

In anguish was Phuong. She battled mightily and repeatedly whacked him in the head with a glass ashtray because she didn't know what else to do. Once, twice, and countless other times

Up until blood smears from his skull covered the white bed...

Her mind was clouded until her tears stopped, and she lost consciousness.

Prior to the phone's ringing, she was unsure of the caller's identity.

Up until An approached her and gave her a hard hug...

Chapter 6

"Pretend sincerity. That's when you stay true to your feelings while talking less about yourself, acting silly, and always remaining confident in yourself".

***

Cong Cafe, Hai Ba Trung, Saigon.

4.00 PM. 2012

Today's sky seemed low and weirdly gray.

Mac smoked a cigarette hesitantly. He turned to face the woman in front of him, raising the collar of his vest.

It had been a long time since he and Ly had been able to sit thus close and gently facing one other. A couple's unusual weekend coffee in the center of Saigon...

A touch unusual, and a little near... He had no idea what to say to Ly.

It was not proper to suggest it was an obligation because he enjoyed spending time with his wife. But to say he was in love was incorrect, for his sentiments had long since vanished.

"Or should we relocate to America?" The atmosphere here was very stuffy for me." Ly abruptly spoke up.

"I don't have much money to go somewhere right now." Should we go back there after you give birth and start over? If it's only for some old memories, I don't think it's worth it..."

"No, I'm not envious of her..."

"What exactly did you say?" And don't refer to Phuong as "that woman." Do you understand why Phuong was not mentioned here? We were a husband and wife team. She was merely an old social acquaintance. That was the case in the past, and it will be the case in the future." Mac felt a twinge of sorrow for his earlier remarks. If Phuong had a chance to hear that, Mac would be at a loss for words.

"Please don't bring that person's name up in front of me. That much explanation is unnecessary. I wouldn't have been so unhappy if you had stopped sooner with this dreadful sensation in your heart."

The environment fell silent once more.

After all, love was not the reason they were together. The squabbles between Ly and Mac would be over soon. He hoped that he and Phuong could bury and leave this feeling behind so that he and Ly could start over. Everything would return to normal as if nothing had happened.

Being young, Mac reasoned, should be uncomplicated, because the complexity of the heart would make everything worse. But there was one thing Mac didn't expect: the wounds of real love would never heal.

***

October 2012

Villa District 7

8.00 PM

Khanh was standing in front of his father's Saigon mansion. He had the impression that the drawing of his dream house that he had submitted to his father had come to life right in front of him. Even though it was his first time here, every detail, every variety of hues felt extremely familiar.

He entered the house peacefully, taking the key that his father had prepared in advance and sent to his mother and son that year. This abandoned house might have made anyone passing by nervous, but not him. Because he imagined and painted this mansion.

Khanh had a peek around the house. His father's approach was undeniably distinct. The paintings were organized according to bizarre criteria that only father and brother knew based on the architecture of the stairway. From when his father taught him to read books, through when both father and son did kick-fit together.

When Khanh played the song "Over and over" from his phone, so many beautiful memories from his past rushed back to him. Strangely, both his father and he liked this song. At the time, he also believed that love might last forever, because he was still dreaming and carefree.

Khanh gazed into the mirror across the hall, his vision clouded.

He hired a housekeeper who came here every weekend to clean. He honored his father by keeping the space where he used to live.

He ascended each floor slowly, inspecting the living room, opening a few drawers, and checking the shelves. He walked into his father's room. Everything remained tidy and clean. His father's favorite fountain pen, inscribed with his name, is still on the table.

"There seemed to be nothing new at all!" Khanh searched the area around him desperately.

Khan shut his eyes. He wanted to sense the ambiance of that evening by putting himself in his father's shoes. He pictured himself in a little room corner. After the company's closing ceremony at the Pullman Hotel, he peered carefully at his father, reading some news and answering emails. However, due to his inebriation, he left the door unlocked. Suddenly, a girl went by that route and entered his house with the goal of robbing property while high on drugs.

An was the name.

However, because his father did not give her any money or drugs, she became enraged, even yelled at her and threatened her, resulting in a temper tantrum, with the goal of killing and exploiting her. The ashtray on the table continuously struck him on the head. She had no idea what was going on until the cops arrived and seized her. The tears, the blood, the sorrow of the other man's family, the meaningless vanity, the instant yearning, and the terrible future of a young girl who had just turned 15 years old marked the conclusion of a very long night.

Khanh blinked his eyes wide. He didn't want to return to this unpleasant past. Was it predetermined by fate if such was the case?

Khanh moaned, two hands cupping his face. He wasn't a cop, he wasn't a detective, and he wasn't a lawyer. He was simply your average film director and producer. How could he possibly be astute enough to discover the truth about his father's death?

Khanh took a look at the fountain pen on the table. This fountain pen, etched with both the letters H.K of his surname, must have been cherished by his father. Khanh fiddled with the pen in his hand, which had an odd button on it.

A few thoughts rushed across his mind. When he was a boy, he frequently observed his father holding multiple pens similar to this one in his father's office. Dad was still recording sessions for reflection and research.

Who knew what else was missing in this place?

Khanh inserted the pen's USB plug into the PC. He listened to each recording in the pen one by one.

One paragraph... two paragraphs... three paragraphs...

Khanh felt a shiver run down his spine. He played back the section he had just heard.

Khanh could feel his eyes burning. His faith in him had all but vanished.

***

January 11, 2013
11:59 p.m.

"You have a pleasant expression. People believe what you say. When I'm with you, I feel at ease and don't feel the need to conceal anything."

Mac awoke in the middle of the night and grinned at the woman sleeping next to him. A dream, it turned out, was still a dream. He didn't know why Phuong kept appearing in his dreams, but the things he uttered to Phuong stayed with him forever.

Mac stated that there were occasions when he discovered he wasn't as good or noble as he thought he was. He still used harmful words, acted carelessly without considering the other party, established material ambitions to live above emotions, and never believed in the luxury of "real love." ".

He had no idea what he was looking for. He nonetheless had a really joyful supper with Ly this afternoon, thinking of a name for their soon-to-be son.

Mac stood up. He jumped out of bed, combed his hair quickly, changed into a good outfit, and crept out of the room. Mac took the perfume aroma that Phuong likes to spritz on his wrist. When Mac glanced at Ly sleeping soundly, he apologized to her numerous times in his mind.

Mac saw himself as unhappy. But he realized that if love was as simple as exchanging and discarding commodities, maybe Mac wouldn't have to suffer as much as he does now.

***

11.45 p.m. January 2013
District 2, Apartment S

The doorbell rang, startling Phuong, who had no idea who had phoned her so late at night. When Phuong opened the door, the man who had planted a complex riddle in her heart was still there.

The same tender kiss. Still the same ravenous hand scouring Phuong's body. There is still the sound of fast breathing. Still the unbreakable hugs, eventually resulting in emotional interference. Only him, gentle but passionate, could bring Phuong such wholeness of mind and body.

When they both realized that this was the final time they may see each other, the music Phuong was playing blended with the sounds of breathing and weeping.

However, Phuong was not pleased this time. The feelings that were creeping all over Phuong were fear and remorse, not love or nostalgia from the past. Mac's shoulder was filled with tears. Phuong abruptly ended the embrace and softly questioned Mac:

"What brought you here so suddenly?"

"Because I know how much I adore you... But I've determined that this is the final time I see you."

"I was going to tell you that as well..."

"I'm sorry, but I'm unable to do anything else. I can't give you any protection, consolation, or safety."

"But do you know what made us fall in love?"

"...I only know that my thoughts are always on you..."

"Partly because we see things in one other that other people don't. I know this is our last night together."

"Do you have another?"

"How come you're asking me that? She is already aware of you and me... She even hired someone to kill me."

When Mac heard Phuong tell the truth, he was taken aback. Mac and Phuong just rubbed their heads together that night, saying nothing. Phuong allowed her sobbing resound, revealing the love hiding in her heart more plainly than ever before, and it was also time to bury it all.

Mac crossed his arms over his brow, still in love, but choosing to give up, not because he didn't love, as someone once said, but simply because this love was not powerful enough to last. Was Ly the person he once loved? What caused her to alter so quickly?

Mac's and Phuong's lives were both empty and lonely. When they found each other, happiness came for a brief moment and then vanished. Perhaps the last moments together were the most beautiful moments each individual had ever experienced throughout their lives.

Obviously, man had no influence over his own destiny. Wouldn't everyone experience remorse, see things become more valuable when there were just a few chances left, or no more tickets to go back?

Was it really so difficult to accept you'd failed in love?

When Mac got out of bed and was preparing to wash his face, he noticed Phuong's photo frame with a child neatly put on the second floor of the bookshelf. When he questioned who the child was, she just joked that it was a grandchild. She grinned brightly in the photo and appeared to be quite happy. This child, on the other hand, had something familiar in the corner of his eye, a mole, and then his innocent smile, which he couldn't understand.

***

Ly kept track of each passing day. She gradually counted down the days till labor began. She couldn't shake the memory of last night, when she pretended to sleep but Mac kept leaving her.

Ly had become the person she had never wanted to be before, relying on her family, settling down with chores, wondering about whether she didn't know where Mac was now, she didn't know if he was happy right now with the girl who stole his heart even if she came first.

She wouldn't have been so perplexed if he had selected her as his life's destination.

Even if she and Mac were now lost together, Ly once dreamed of a grand love without calculating, hatred, or guilt. People stated that what was so good sounded unreal, and it was true because many times such thing didn't exist.

Mac had lost interest in her.

Mac was the type of person that lived recklessly with his emotions. She obviously couldn't transform a person or modify the foundation of a personality.

Ly sat by herself in the room. Looking in the mirror, she wondered how long she could maintain her attractiveness.

She remembered Mac telling her that if she wasn't content with the world around her, she should look in the mirror and ask herself who she was and why she had come to this life.

Li was completely clueless. Ly just knew that her prior loving gestures, her previous concern for the person she loved, were now a thing of the past.

She remembered Mac proposing to her. The two sat at the familiar Cong cafe on a cold wet day in Hanoi. He knelt, took out his ring, and placed it on her finger. Ly was overjoyed that day. Her smile lingered on her lips indefinitely.

At the moment, her happiness was something she didn't need to produce or keep. However, it turned out that she was the only one who thought so.

During their days together, she relied on him to cry, laugh, express her grief, and seek comfort and protection. However, all Ly received in return was apathy and mute rage, just because neither of them had faith in their love adventure.

Ly kept telling herself that she couldn't stop. She couldn't allow that girl take away the person she cared about. What was wrong with her fighting, even becoming a little selfish to keep her small family happy?

***

“Today is a beautiful day”. Phuong reminded herself that the weather in Saigon was rarely as pleasant as it was in Hanoi. Saigon was always bustling and rapid, and everything was rushed at times, causing individuals to forget what they truly required.

But what if we were all after the same thing?

In Saigon, Phuong was surrounded by the most terrifying fears, darkest regrets, and even the most irrational aspirations.

"Never leave the house in anything less than a $1,000 outfit."

Phuong had made it a goal since becoming the Communications Director of a huge technology business to never leave the house wearing a suit that cost so much.

Although Phuong understood in her heart that this luxury made no sense, if not seemed ludicrous. But what to do when people had become accustomed to living in a world where appearance was already the criterion by which most individuals were judged?

Professionalism had to take the place of chastity and purity. Wearing a white outfit and black pointed clogs. The gray handbag and shoes from the same brand were also fairly appropriate.

Phuong had a date with a very special woman today. It could be claimed that she was someone Phuong could not ignore or dismiss. She was Mac's wife. Despite her lack of beauty, she appeared to be easy on the eyes and determined. More importantly, she separated Mac from the other girls in terms of rank.

Saigon was not a difficult place to live in, but it was extremely tough when people were preoccupied with things other than love.

Phuong approached the table in the cafe's secret corner. Despite her lack of makeup, the 29-year-old woman standing in front of Phuong projected confidence and unusual strength.

"Can you tell me what you want me to do today?"

"I want you and Mac to come to a total halt."

"We called it quit a long time ago."

"We? End? When did the two of you get close enough to be referred to as "us"?

"How many times do I need to explain to you before you're satisfied?" Why have you come to visit me if the ring on your finger is truly yours?"

"What?"

"You're terrified, aren't you? That silver ring suits my style better. You can only keep Mac due to the child! Don't be too arrogant about your position!".

"You..." Ly attempted to keep her rage inside. "Do you know why I came to see you today in person?"

"I wouldn't have come to meet you if I hadn't known." I see no reason to disagree with you. He, like any other man, chose the safe route."

"Shut up... My husband and I didn't eat together because of you. He no longer asked how I was, and he no longer made the same affectionate gestures that he used to."

"..."

"I notice him being exhausted all the time. We pass each other on a daily basis, but he always keeps his secret. I'm curious what I know about him. Clearly, not much."

"But that's your problem."

Phuong smiled and smoked a cigarette to relax. She hadn't smoked in a long time. The males surrounding her didn't enjoy it, so she had to "fake deer" in order to give up her "favorite" meal.

"Why would you hire someone to kill me if you're a decent person? Are you the only woman Mr. Mac ever loved? "Does begging for someone elsc's adoration make sense?"

"Don't be so arrogant so quickly... You never know what will happen tomorrow."

Phuong laughed; Ly was a woman who was never content with what she had or pushed by life. She wished to object. Perhaps Ly believed that pushing others into the abyss would make her feel better.

Phuong went out of the cafe. She stood there watching the passing cars, her sorrow reaching a peak. She used to have no one to celebrate her victories with, and she now had no one to console her when she was lonely.

Chapter 7

"Sometimes you have to admit that you blew an opportunity and it's too late to change your mind."

January 2013,

8.30 PM

Khanh's house

Music was playing throughout the room. A dazzling and gorgeous chandelier hung above the ceiling, seemingly directly in front of the eyes yet unable to be approached, just like its owner.

Khanh was one of these people. Khanh was on high alert and wouldn't let anyone get too close.

He was with Phuong in this room. There were only two persons. Phuong forced her mouth to open, shattering the dreadful silence:

"I've been expecting you for a long time. Can you also jump right to the primary topic?"

"Do you like wine? Chardonnay or Zinfandel?" Khanh simply poured the drink and grinned.

"Whatever. I'm not as knowledgeable as you."

Khanh sipped his drink. He lit a cigarette, took a deep breath, and then stared Phuong in the eyes:

"Thank you for delivering me the most recent script..."

"How are you feeling...?"

"Honestly, that work... isn't special enough to be made into a film."

"... What exactly do you mean?"

"Don't give up so easily." There are numerous options."

"So, what exactly do you want me to do?"

"The quality of the script is not required to make a movie that is on fire."

"..."

"How can you assist me with this?" I'm an investor, so I need something to ensure that I'll be lucrative after doing business with you."

Phuong laughed. She had brought nothing with her when she came here to talk to him.

They met in an elevator and on Tinder, and both times he stopped her when she was about to be stabbed and sexually harassed. Episodes from Korean movies that she had seen on the internet were suddenly unfolding in her real life.

Phuong paused:

"I'm out of options." Only I."

"Do you believe I like you?"

"You can still think of me..."

Phuong had just done speaking and was going to turn away when Khanh drew her back and kissed her on the lips. What made this circumstance seem so familiar? She felt like she'd had a deja vu moment somewhere. In the dream, the gray-painted room remained, as did the sensation of resisting someone. Something flashed across her mind at this point, a peculiar emotion she didn't want to recall.

Phuong involuntarily jumped up and pulled Khanh away with her hand after experiencing ecstasy when caressing a man's lips:

"Damn you. Is this my chance to become famous?"

"Ha ha, how are you feeling?" Do you understand the concept of "love without conditions"?

" ... "

"$20.000 each date, not to mention I will gradually introduce you to a partner, so you may do business with me."

"I'm not a slacker." Phuong unintentionally growled.

"The issue isn't the background or societal title, nor is it the script's quality or lack thereof... My brand's problem is a director named Huy Khanh..."

" ... "

"... I'll make a film based on your script." I will give this film my all. Let's just say it's the money you give to the film's production every time you date me."

"Do you really like me that much?" "Do you constantly pay to date girls?"

"Not really... It's just... "I'm a little interested in you."

"How can I put my trust in you?" What happened to the contract? What happened to the signature? "What type of business makes promises by word of mouth?"

"It is true that the Communications Director of Vietnam's biggest technological business. Talking is always clear, and the mind is always clear..."

Khanh stopped speaking and placed the $20.000 check on the dining table, defiantly staring at Phuong.

"Women who are so intelligent are not always popular. I don't need to sign a long contract; I only need you to act now, right?"

***

He texted Phuong more since the day they met at Khanh's residence. Although there was no affection and it was simply a symbiotic relationship, Phuong felt less empty and lonely when someone texted her every day.

Phuong still convinced herself that she needed money and that she wanted to be famous; she didn't want to live a life of plowing and working all day, doing things she was no longer thrilled about.

On the first day of dating Khanh, Phuong went to a pub with sizzling music, just the way she liked it, but in her mind, she still had feelings for Mac. Khanh took Phuong's hand in his and strolled into the pub, softly hugging her every time a stranger walked by, letting her lie in his arms and feel his warmth.

The two went to see the movie debut at the most prestigious theatre in town on the second day. Phuong despised viewing romance movies, but Khanh enjoyed them. What else could Phuong do as someone who had staked his reputation on this "commercial deal"? Phuong didn't feel completely at ease with Khanh. Khanh exaggerated his own importance. He always assumed that what he stated was the greatest, and that it was the best for each individual.

Phuong went to Khanh's private house without any precautions on the third day. She had no idea why she had decided to be so daring. Khanh played a violin concerto from the 1990s for her to hear and talked about topics he had never shared: his goals, his ex-lovers, his days growing up without a father but always with his mother's encouragement.

In the midst of his emotions, Khanh began to give Phuong loving kisses, but Phuong responded erratically. The two sank into the passions of two individuals without love. Phuong had no idea she and Khanh would get this far.

However, until Khanh began to unbutton the first buttons, Phuong's eyes awoke with the image of that 5-year-old youngster in his thoughts. She began pushing Khanh away once more.

Despite Khanh's voice pursuing her, she ran out from that house as soon as reason returned.

Her head hurt like hell. She didn't want to think about the past, which had left her unable to eat, sleep, or act normally for a long time.

In the days that followed, Phuong requested for a leave of absence from the company, working discreetly from home. Her thoughts kept reliving that night all day. It wasn't that Khanh did anything wrong to Phuong, or that she was horrified by it; it was just that her conscience wouldn't allow it.

Because the boy was always in her brain, because there was no love between her and Khanh, and because she found herself living more and more casually. She didn't let herself live by her feelings because she didn't want to forget what had made her who she was today, even if she didn't know what that meant.

Phuong sent a message a few days later to break her relationship with Khanh. She thought her time with Khanh was exquisite, but it wasn't enough to keep her going. Despite the fact that her reputation was crucial, she refused to address it with Khanh.

This was a barter connection. End. She stopped sinking deep and developing feelings for others.

Khanh, contrary to her expectations, reacted calmly. He nonetheless agreed to direct a film based on her script. She didn't understand why he did it; the script wasn't as good as he'd said. Obviously, the two had no unique bond. Or was she the only one who felt this way?

He'd realize one day that their supposedly intimate friendship had been built on a misconception.

He would one day open his eyes wide and see that she was not worthy of his adoration.

Phuong gradually fell asleep while listening to old music she used to listen to on the phone with her father. This love was so brief, but why did Phuong have an uneasy feeling?

Phuong sighed when he heard the faint hum of the ceiling fan. *Afflictions in love, after all, were only there because we already had an answer in our hearts. But, in reality, that answer was too painful to confront, therefore we didn't want to or know how to confront it.*

ʎ ʎ ʎ

Mac sipped a Rosemary drink at the well-known Bar Betta at the start of the alley. The present weather in Saigon made Mac long for Hanoi. Even if he visited every nook and cranny of this town, Mac would never feel as at ease as he did in his birthplace.

Mac used to always listen to his parents about everything: where he went to school, who his friends' children were, and who he played with. He knew he'd gone the boring safe road, but taking risks wasn't always the best option for him.

His parents were ordinary federal officials, since they were concerned about their children and didn't want them to fall behind their peers, Mac's parents gritted their teeth and spent money so that he could attend schools that were both affordable and well-known in their country. Although this was not Mac's favorite career, living in a country where society valued degrees, it was worth acquiring a couple more degrees to easily move ahead in society.

Mac had a vision. Mac wanted to draw and wished to create cartoons, but he lacked the talent to draw and wasn't strong enough to do so on his own. So, at the age of 27, after returning from studying in the United Kingdom, Mac had the insane idea of making animated short films for social networks.

Mac asked his younger brother in high school to draw for him and pay for his bills as a long-term seasonal contract because he couldn't draw. Mac bought his work and his name. He was exclusively in charge of the script. Mac let him do it all, from drawing to video to editing. Mac just liked "money to give oatmeal," regardless of whether he was happy with it. He was eager to do so whether it was renowned or not, perhaps because he wanted money to cover his life and also to forget the sad things that had just transpired.

He came to see Mac at the most vital time, Mac remembered. His father had recently died, his mother was unwell once more, and his lover huddled in a corner as he watched his family break apart. He once loved her with all his heart, once turned down a job offer from a well-known firm to attend a performance with her, once spent the weekend at the movies, comforting her. After seeing a poignant Korean film, he once purchased her an LV bag with a few months' pay to make her "equal to pals." But in the end, she dated someone else because his family became bankrupt, he gained weight unexpectedly, and he no longer looked as "fit" as before because he didn't have enough time to exercise and take care of himself.

After a few years, she invested in a cosmetic project that failed, and the guy she was dating moved on with someone else. But she ended up marrying someone who was richer, more gorgeous, younger, and more spoiled. Her temperament was such that the end result was to toss it away, and her heart rarely housed the concept of love.

It was true that sometimes you didn't know what you'd just played until you got off the stage. Break up and you'll know if it was love or not.

Mac had stopped believing in love or anything else since then. Wasn't the appearance everything in this "sticky flesh" life? Clothes created a monk, and who could tell a criminal from a businessman if he didn't display his back but only his outer vest?

During that time, Mac's animated short film project drew the attention of the press, and Mac was also referred to as entering showbiz. Even if he couldn't draw, he was nonetheless well-liked in the movies. In his heart, Mac simply saw them as dumb, but in the end, Mac grew tired of that world of illusory titles. Mac had moments when he realized he didn't live for what he liked, but only to be recognized as someone who knew what to do, wear, play, and act like. *The sense of right and wrong was frequently secondary to how other people perceived you. And the distinction between artifice and inventiveness was sometimes simply determined by acting talent.*

The more he conformed to society's expectations, the more Mac became a stranger in his own life. He gradually lost faith in himself and his ideals. Ly was standing next to Mac at the time. Seven years ago, the two met while he was on vacation in Vietnam and instantly fell in love like two moths. Ly awoke feelings in him that other women could not, and she also made significant sacrifices for him. But Mac's parents refused to accept Ly, and he had little motive to persuade them other than his love for her.

Ly and Mac's sentiments of sadness were protracted. After two years of dating, the couple split up, and the animated short film project became a "bomb," a downward trend. The brother who worked with Mac no longer wanted to sketch. This universe was insane. You would quickly fade into obscurity if you did not adapt to the necessities of society. Mac was also among the losers.

Following that endeavor, Mac went on to get a master's degree in marketing in the United Kingdom. Mac picked Marketing since he didn't know what he enjoyed other than making short films, which was only a transitory interest.

Mac merely wanted to be the greatest in his field; any industry would suffice as long as he could live, as long as he had a future, and most importantly, he didn't want to ponder too much.

The gifted Mac's younger brother chose to study in France. Mac just spoke to him on the phone because he had been out of touch with him for a long time owing to a traffic accident. He also did not allow Mac to visit for fear of disturbing him, despite the fact that he never thought so.

Mac ran into Ly again after returning from England after 5 years. Although they were no longer overjoyed with each other, both of them made an unintentional error in an inebriated state due to their shallowness. Ly was expecting his first child. Ly was also in debt with her ex-lover at the time. During their courtship, Ly borrowed money from him to care for her mother's illness and feed her younger siblings. Mac realized that at the time, Ly had no other option because she couldn't care for the entire family on her own.

After all, Mac chose to live in Saigon with Ly. To begin. Leave nothing behind.

Mac began "earning his keep" in this place by teaching Marketing. Although tedious, Mac had a steady job at the center that paid the bills for the entire family. After all, life revolved only around the rice-clothing-rice-money cycle, and there was no need for pity. Whoever was stronger would triumph, and the weak would just be substitutes for paving the way, as the adage "Strong wins, weak loses" implies.

Mac drank the glass of wine on the table, looking at the back and forth of the street, wondering what would have happened if he had listened to his parents, lived in Hanoi, and worked as a prestigious Marketing Director that day. Although Mac did not come here because he loved Ly, despite the fact that she used to treat him very well, and despite the fact that the two had a 7-year relationship and had a child together. However, that positive sensation was not always enough to keep him going. Perhaps because Ly was not the woman of his dreams.

The two appeared to have planned their split. The distinctions that once graced family life become a pretext for rage and never-ending squabbles.

Perhaps both Mac and Ly are too naive to believe that young love can overcome all obstacles and change the disparities that are intrinsic hurdles.

However, life was too hard with that passion of both.

Mac was aware that he had also missed an appointment with another female. Even though she was 5 years younger than him at the time, she was the one who shook him up from his delusions and showed him what he needed. Age didn't reveal much. Mac remembered her perplexed eyes, sloppy smile, and the times she told him jokes. That naivety stayed with him for the rest of his life. Mac, on the other hand, gave up on her because he lacked the fortitude to leave his safe reality. Until then, when they reconnected, he found his love as strong as ever.

When you were in love, no matter how far away you were, your heart felt extremely close. Mac and Phuong were too close, too acquainted, to notice the obvious chill when they were with another person.

Mac laughed as the harsh salty water ran down his cheeks, since this life had too many games that he was obliged to play even if he didn't want to.

"Ting" - Mac was shocked by the message's sound. It was Phuong's message. Still a question to visit, and he hoped the start of the week was as productive as usual. Phuong was always delicate and compassionate. She had a sweetness and understanding that few girls possessed. Although Mac desperately wanted to see her again, he wanted to tell her that he was foolish not to embrace her feelings, and that he was overjoyed that she had been taken into an unknown realm. However, things did not appear to proceed as planned. If she continued, Mac would only bring her misery.

We had to realize that we had blown an opportunity and that it was too late to turn back.

Mac was about to return home after finishing the final drops of the cocktail when he received a call from an unknown number. Mac heard a voice on the other end of the line that was both familiar and foreign, both inviting and threatening:

"Hello, Mac, how have you been? "Do you remember my voice?"

***

Chapter 8

"In our efforts to demonstrate our superiority, we forget that we, too, are human."

Mac's eyes were dilated, and the corners of his mouth were smeared in blood from brutal blows. Mac had no idea this day would come so swiftly.

The phone began to play "Blowing in the Wind," causing Mac to appear to awaken after the killing strikes. It was Ly's decision. The melancholy whistling in the background music tormented him for the rest of his life. Mac, as usual, allowed melancholy to cling to his heart. It was him, Ly's ex-boyfriend, the towering figure with platinum-dyed hair and tattooed arms. He inquired of Mac:

"When are you going to pay me?"

"Please give me a couple more weeks!"

"So, when you stole Ly from me that day, where were you waiting for me?" Will you give me some space?"

" ... "

"At first, I was going to let it go... But, given that Ly owes me a lot of money to maintain her family, what is this worth in comparison to what she's already dug for me?"

"Don't refer to Ly as "it." ". I promise to repay Ly's debt. Only a few weeks left."

"How many weeks are there left?" Promises that fall flat? What you study in books cannot be applied in conversation, Master! Why do you have to put up with it? All you have to do is give over Ly to me. Isn't it best, men, to deal with it as soon as possible?"

"However, Ly is my wife. "How can I be so careless!"

"Irresponsible? So, are you certain the child in Ly's womb is yours?"

"Stop talking right now!"

Mac's foot kicked straight into the stomach of Ly's ex-lover as he protested out of control. When the other two men saw this, they did not hesitate to beat the dust with an iron rod, giving Mac a couple harsh kicks in the stomach. He attempted to fight back, but was sent to the ground by another blow to the middle of his face. Blood poured from his mouth, leaving lengthy trails on Mac's torso. Ly's ex-lover grinned and patted Mac on the back of the head with his hand. His voice was clear, and his words were menacing:

"I GIVE YOU TWO WEEKS MORE. Deliver half of the debt each week!"

Having stated that, the other two juniors let go of Mac's hand, leaving him alone in the open field, and the three of them went. How did Mac earn 1 billion VND in a single week? He couldn't raise his hand to plead with his parents. Ly didn't have any money either, so he volunteered to be her replacement. Mac couldn't even ask Phuong. She'd been so wonderful to him, she'd made too many sacrifices for him to beg or ask for aid.

Mac concealed his melancholy behind his eyelashes whenever he thought of Phuong. Mac was not a lover, and he did not give up all for love. But there was always pain in him when both he and the other side opted to leave each other because of "career" and "duty." Mac had no idea of hating someone, reminiscing about his youth, or squandering anything. *If you were to blame, you should blame yourself for being too weak and insecure to hold your loved one's hand through the trials of life.*

Mac closed his eyes while holding his head with both hands. He desired to be free of the burdensome reality. He was too fatigued to continue walking on the lengthy trip. He cleaned the blood stains from his mouth and nose with the sleeve of his shirt, while his white shirt was now stained with dark red from the beating, with bloodshot brows, puffy lips, and puffy eyes in a few moments ago

Because the signal was weak, the taxi call didn't have a good signal, and it was difficult for a cab across the street to trust him to transport him home with such a bad look.

Mac grinned. People encircled him and smiled at him when he was happy. When he was alone, not even a shadow could be seen.

Mac saw himself involuntarily becoming a disaster and no longer a glimmer of hope in the middle of this desolate road, with no one going by. The brilliant light from the oncoming automobile stunned Mac as he sat on the pavement. The man in the automobile lowered the window gradually. Mac frowned, wearing the same familiar striped shirt, clever specs, and attentive gaze. Something made him pause. Maybe his joy in life wasn't ended yet, or maybe it was just getting started.

"Can you get in the car?" I don't think you'll be able to last much longer!" Slyly, said the man with the smart glasses.

***

Ly's tears were gently falling in the middle of the black space, as were

Phuong's mournful eyes and the platinum-haired oligarch's frightening grin. They gathered Mac, approached him, wiped the belated tears from his eyes, and suddenly everything faded into nothingness.

There was nothing but deep dark emptiness around Mac, no way out, no salvation. He kept running, but he never knew when to leave this place. Mac awoke with the harsh fluorescent lights of the hospital in front of him, surrounded by four blue walls. The light made him dizzy unconsciously, so he leaned against the bed to calm himself.

In recent years, Mac had felt as if he was living but simply walking beside life, mired in disillusionment and delusion with his long-lost old love.

Mac believed that by obtaining a Master's degree, he would be able to cover all of his responsibilities to Phuong. But his life, like so many others, was precarious. Could anyone relate to him?

He couldn't do anything else with Ly - his wife. The kid in Ly's womb was the one thing that could bring two souls who had lost touch back together. He didn't live solely for the sake of his heart, but partly because his intellect taught him that love was not a panacea.

"Do you think you're awake?" The man in spectacles has just begun to talk.

"You are..."

"It's me. In the past, you followed me everywhere."

"When did you come back to Vietnam, you?" When Mac saw Khanh's picture materialize in front of him, he was startled that he didn't say anything. "You're so different... "I didn't realize."

"I've also been back for a few months since I've been too busy, so I didn't check the emails you sent. And how do you explain this scenario to yourself? I believed you were going to break some ribs since your eyes and mouth were so swollen."

"It's difficult to say... about my family."

Mac struggled to find a pack of smokes and a lighter as soon as he finished speaking when he discovered everything in his pocket had been thrown into a nearby trash can. Khanh lifted his eyelashes slightly as he observed Mac's anguish:

"What are you smoking now?" You can't do anything if you don't stay healthy."

"So you believe you're more stronger than I do?" Mac adoration. "After five years of not seeing you, you've changed a lot."

"Haha, I recognized the mole on your eye right away." We've been separated for so long, since I was 18, 19. And who are these folks, and do you have enough money to pay for them?"

"Ly and I are married. And it was Ly's ex-lover right now." Mac exhaled heavily. "In the past, Ly would borrow a huge sum of money from him to pay for his mother's cancer surgery and to care for his younger brothers."

"But why do you have to keep hiding for her?" This is not your fault."

"It's because Ly is my wife." I can't give them Ly. He could not, however, afford such a considerable sum of money. I had no idea I'd run across you in this situation."

"It is true that the situation is not ideal." Khanh made a tongue-clicking motion.

"And what about you?"

"All I have is work." But I'm in love with a female. I'm delighted I regained my emotions."

"Congratulations. Finally, someone has the power to alter you."

"I used to think that people wouldn't give me anything good besides always harming me, but that girl was really weird... Unfortunately, everything between us was "broken." It's been a long time..."

Mac tried to keep his surprise at the sight of that female on Khanh's phone to himself. Khanh caught Mac's eye. Khanh's black eyes indicated his joy when he mentioned that girl, despite his sorrowful voice. Wasn't that the person Mac had been thinking about for quite some time?

It was often difficult to comprehend that the earth was so round. People were sometimes dissatisfied because they believed everything revolved around them and tried to change things that were not in their control.

*** **Hoai Nam Hair Salon, District 1**

8.10 PM

Ann looked at the time. It was after 8 p.m. An was fatigued because of the chemical odor and the scattered curls of hair on the floor.

An had been working at this hair salon near Phuong's residence for a week. Haircutting, curling, dying, and shampooing for guests was not a challenging profession, but the pay was fairly good compared to what An used to "scratch and peel" to apply for a piercing. What he learned in prison was also extremely beneficial to An. There was still something that An couldn't feel passionate about.

Fate was only the fault of those who refused to accept responsibility for their own lives. How liberated were we in our lives? How many times had An asked himself that question and been unable to find an answer?

An returned home along the familiar passageway after the shift. An leaped down the alley under the moonlight, the shadow of the trees engraved on it. An recalled how he and Phuong used to wander the way home from extra classes. They were more closer back then than they were now.

People seemed to drift apart from one another as we grew older, didn't they? Because of "rice and money," celebrity, status, or simply because they no longer wanted to be together. Everyone appeared to want to go far, but what was happening in front of them appeared to be more appealing.

Phuong was not the same then as she was now. Phuong frequently talked, laughed, or confided in her worries. She was frail because she was very sensitive. She taught herself that no one had the right to hurt her except herself. Even whether it was something as insignificant as having to face low grades, seeing her alone in high school strolling with other people, or waiting until her father died, Phuong was driven to commit suicide.

However, Phuong simply thought about it and did not act on it. She did it because she knew she had to survive. She wasn't devoted to what she had, and she didn't want her life to be boring.

In An's opinion, Phuong relied on suffering to survive, allowing melancholy to gnaw at her throughout the day. But An was confident that she would make it. Phuong was nice and talented, and she inspired others to believe in their skills.

Phuong's life was unusual. Her happiness was little, frail, and easily broken. Phuong rarely felt it completely. An also desired to bring joy into her life in order to assist her, but she appeared to have established a very strong boundary with An, preventing him from penetrating any deeper.

An was still there, but he was invisible and couldn't exist in Phuong's eyes.

Looking down the street at the crowded businesses, when would he be able to return to the days of true calm, he wondered?

"What the hell is a friend?" "Friends are only there to help each other, right?"

An came to a halt as he heard a familiar voice. He took a look around. It was only the space of a popular barbecue restaurant in the neighborhood, but who was this with the curling chestnut brown hair, sad eyes, high nose bridge, and vivid orange lips? In addition to the girl An had been secretly admiring for a long time?

An had always seen Phuong from a distance before she recognized An existed. Perhaps it was just because An couldn't provide her with what she truly required.

An approached the pub, plainly observing the surrounding men's interested eyes on the girl sitting alone among a series of drinks on the table. An took a seat next to Phuong at the table. Phuong's eyes were hazy, and her cheeks were flushed. Phuong gently smiled as she leaned on An's shoulder:

"So you've already arrived? Why do you always appear when I'm the most tired?"

***

Phuong hadn't been able to look An in the eyes like this in a long time. The surroundings were nothing magical, simply a run-of-the-mill wayside pub.

"Why have you avoided me for the past few days?" Phuong asked, taking a sip of the traditional Saigon beer.

"From whom am I hiding?" Ann burst out laughing. "You're just too preoccupied to notice me!"

"Did you hear what I heard?" Phuong began to cry. "For the past ten years, I've never stopped wondering if you ate well, slept well,... I never thought I deserved to be with you."

" ... "

"I lack the confidence to confront your tolerance!" Even though I attempted to live up to your expectations..."

"Why do you need to think so hard? It's OK". An said. "I forgot about everything!"

An wiped the wetness that was dripping from Phuong's eyes with his hand. It had been a long time since they had been able to sit across from one other and express their feelings.

The two exchanged stories about their initial days together. An recalled the first time Phuong was mistakenly moved to An's school. The two sat next to one other on the bus for the first time. An recalled how they were both reprimanded by the sisters for harassing and singing in a serious place when they both went to church. An recalled how they had both purchased cotton pots to offer to each other on New Year's Day.

An also vividly remembered the first few days they had spent in Saigon. This great city had assisted both of them in having unforgettable times when saving every silver coin to drink coffee at beautiful cafes, have delicious dishes at costly restaurants, or experience the weird sense of being in a restaurant dancing under the magical lights at the bar. He still recalled many, many...

Those recollections gradually grew up and silently obediently persisted both in An's memory and in Phuong's continual smile, as if it were just yesterday. They were friends once, and they would always be friends, a priceless notion.

An understood Phuong was fatigued not only because of An, but also because she had been under too much pressure to live up to her feelings for far too long. Phuong talked about Mac, Khanh, and the most lonely periods, even though An had no idea what that person named Khanh looked like. It was said that Phuong slept with guys in order to have someone to support her career as a scriptwriter, and that Phuong got up simply by doing that rag job.

People gossiped about Phuong's private life like they were laying under the bed. An only needed to know that it was Phuong, the girl he was always keeping an eye on, who had the best option. Because, truly, who could know what was best for the person they loved?

Chapter 9

Hoai Nam Hairsalon, District 1

8 p.m., January 2013

"Please, next guest." An smiled as a customer entered the store. "What kind of service do you want to provide?"

"I want to cut my hair like I've just fallen in love." Half-joking, half-true. "I agree that what kind of haircut makes me more gorgeous than my ex."

Ann burst out laughing. He also experienced a few guests with volatile moods from time to time:

"I'll cut what I believe looks best on you."

"It's all up to you." Ha gently examined herself in the mirror opposite.

"Please let me have some coffee. I'm thirsty!"

"Sure". An offered Ha a cup of coffee at the salon. "Have a good time."

Ha sipped her drink. Although Ha's head was heavy with previous problems, this cup of coffee was like blowing them away. This coffee tasted unusual and not at all boring. It was a new kind of brew that Ha, a coffee enthusiast, had never tried before.

"Would you mind showing me how to create this drink? I'm also a coffee fanatic, but I've never tried it." Ha spoke out with a knowing tone.

"This recipe is also a "heirloom, as my grandma used to do it for me when I was a child."

"Don't worry, just tell me a little about it. I'll treat you to a celebratory meal!" Ha chuckled.

Ha and An have been texting one other more since that day. An and Ha had two common interests: coffee and music. They could talk about coffee all day without growing tired of it. They discussed building a shop, different types of coffee, how to make them, and the layout of the coffee shops they had both visited. Ha also planned to become a singer at the bar by hosting Acoustic sessions on weekends. Just like that, one story after another, their friendship became closer as a result.

An was obsessed with the insignificant. Listening to music played by the neighbors in the afternoon, stumbling onto a good book, or even receiving a funny message from Ha was enough to keep An pleased all day.

An had no desire to become a "superman" in the eyes of others through a gigantic career since he knew that no matter how great he was, he couldn't cling to them when he was alone.

An didn't want to end up like Phuong. He couldn't understand why she saw life as an endless war. An had lost track of what she had been fighting for.

***

Spark Club, Saigon, 11.30 p.m.

Saturday evening. Spark was as usual engrossed in the colorful lights. An gave Ha a friendly smile. There was something special about this girl that made him want to know her for the rest of his life. Although Ha did not appear to be overly excellent, was not overly brilliant, and was even somewhat plain and pragmatic, there was something unnecessary, honest, and uncalculated - lost in Ha. An initial impression was that with a person like her, who was largely vulnerable to males, she would have to slip a lot more times before she could mature.

An let his mind wander amid the music. An no longer allowed his head to act on feelings. He was continually thinking, thinking, thinking. As a result, when he and Phuong were together, there was never a void. That priceless tranquility had become increasingly scarce. People generally believed that love was for entertainment, but An couldn't figure out why he couldn't grin when he saw Phuong anymore.

Contrary to the myriad of thoughts racing through An's mind, Ha began conversing with a few males flirting around. Perhaps the tight-fitting, half-sleeved black dress had finally done the trick. That was it; she knew how to make herself appealing and how to utilize her charm to achieve her aims, whether they were as simple as "getting to bed" with a man or "digging" him if required.

It had been a long time since Ha had felt so important and surrounded by so many people. She had lost her desire for love after leaving Minh Nhat. She'd had a lot of adventures, but having someone emerge out of nowhere to gain her trust was difficult. There was always the thought of comparing the new to the old, despite the fact that she was well aware that competition would never be healthy, at least to her emotions.

A man with a black jacket approached Ha from the distance. He looked fantastic in a Saint Laurent outfit. He presented Ha with a light gin and tonic cocktail.

"Are you a hybrid?"

"How come you say that?"

"You're really lovely, but you're not Vietnamese; your beauty was inherited from the Philippines and Vietnam!"

"Thanks. You look great in that nice jacket."

"Really?... Just you at here?"

"No. My best friend goes with me. My name is Ha, and this is An." Ha started dragging An into the conversation.

"...My name is Khanh, and it's a pleasure to meet you two."

Ha's eyes shone with delight as he held Khanh's hand. Khanh kissed Ha on the cheek. They both knew it was going to be a memorable evening. An, on the other hand, simply took a sip of the medicine.

Whatever happened, happened. Khanh took Ha home with him. Khanh exclaimed after some foreplay and violent lovemaking. He smiled and looked at Ha, his hand stroking every line of her face.

"Tonight is fantastic... Is there anything genuine between you and him?"

"He? You mean An? I met him at a barbershop near my house, and An isn't really a man... "Do you know who he is?"

"No. He just appears to be familiar. I believe I've seen him before..."

"An has a criminal history." However, this was due to a few earlier errors. You wouldn't condemn someone based on their past, would you?"

"Ignore it. So you're solely concerned about... am I correct?"

"Haha, you're so sure of yourself. Anyway, being a non-binding lover is enjoyable. We'll get to know one other better after tonight."

Khanh and Ha continued to spend many more nights together after that day. As sweet as it was, they both understood that this physical connection would soon come to an end. Ha didn't know if it was deliberate or unintentional, or if it was because Ha confided in Khanh or because his exploiting talent was good, but Khanh knew more and more about An every day.

After the thrill of a Saturday night, Khanh impulsively opened:

"You should get rid of An."

"What's the matter?" Are you envious?"

"Jealous? Who do you believe I am to be envious of? We are simply a love relationship with no strings attached. You're free to leave me anytime you meet someone you truly adore. He's just not deserving of your friendship!"

"Unworthy? So, what is it worth?"

"An was in prison and was a drug addict. You have to know how to protect yourself. He was a dangerous adolescent criminal. Who knows if he'll get high one day and commit the same crime?"

"No. An has never experienced any health issues. Except for the case that year, An never used methamphetamine again. I studied An's old health records, and now he wants to work as an apprentice at the Z. cafe near my house!"

"It's just paper in the end." Papers can be forged; don't presume you know everything."

"I don't think you're all that bright either."

"Have you ever slept with him before? Are you hard on yourself"

Khanh smirked as he felt Ha's hard slap. Ha sobbed. She dressed hurriedly and left the house. She didn't want to keep talking to a patriarchal guy and belittling others like Khanh. Yes, she felt feelings for him even though they only dated for a brief time. His stare, his presence, and his listening all emitted a magnetism that made Ha flutter, making her feel safe and wanting to confess all her heart's concerns.

"Goodbye, my three-week lover!" Ha simply carried a Gucci bag and walked out of the room gently.

Khanh laughed as he watched Ha's figure fade behind the door. Ha was more than just the Cinderella figure from the fairy tale; this time she left him before midnight.

Khanh was unable to conceal his feelings of resentment. In his mind, he always wanted to corner An and find out all of his faults. But he had to restrain himself. Nobody had any idea who he was. He could only wait for his turn because he had lost faith in justice for a long time...

... The moment when the truth was revealed.

Chapter 10

Khanh was cuddled up on the bed with a wool blanket. He peered out the window at the little raindrops. Another wet day in Saigon. He grinned as he sipped some Strongbow cider, remembering what it was like to love someone.

Although he appeared to be quite calm and steady, Khanh frequently glanced at the coffee shop he and Phuong used to frequent while walking down the street, often feeling apprehensive whether going to the movies alone or passing a few moments with the girls who have the same Phuong's hair and body form.

This Saigon was so odd that even when he felt at home, he recognized he didn't belong anyplace.

Khanh has recently invested in producing films based on Phuong's script. He believed he could forget everything. He went to the movies every day, hardly stopping to talk or sleep. To prevent the melancholy that follows a long day, he must find a method to sleep soundly or date and play lightly with a few girls in order to forget his misery. One of them was Ha.

Khanh knew that if Phuong was alright, everything would be fine. Phuong, with her strong personality, always knew how to make herself happy. However, Khanh understood that even if the two part ways, it did not signify the end of what was.

So, as a matter of nature, we didn't require anyone's counsel in love affairs. It was like we were adults; we stopped crying every time we got vaccinated.

Khanh yearned for Phuong. That nostalgia reminded him of how much he missed Hanoi's winter. He went through every Phuong-related article on the internet. He went over every detail to make sure he understood every time and milestone in her life. He had the impression that he cared more for this woman than he did about himself at times.

Khanh convinced himself numerous times that he had no affections for Phuong and that he only came to Phuong for sexual reasons. But deep down, he felt he needed more from Phuong. He couldn't get her nice greeting and bashful grin out of his head. Khanh did not make a sacrifice for Phuong because he believed that such a special girl would never emerge in this world again.

Khanh had a flashback to Minh Ngoc, the girl who had harmed him a few years earlier. Obviously, when she said goodbye, he didn't believe the two of them had ended their relationship; he thought it was just a temporary separation. But Khanh was mistaken. His love story was the same as everyone else's, with no exceptions or last-minute surprises. He used to be too naive to believe that simply giving love would result in the same in return.

"Don't let anyone "teach life" a lesson in sacrifice to me". Khanh was overcome with grief as he reflected on the events of the past. Khanh went to great lengths to gain the respect of that girl. But what exactly did Minh Ngoc do? She used it as an excuse to leave him, "poisoning" his spirit with damned love clichés. She left him because his family went bankrupt and he was in a car accident. She was tired of him, didn't want to be with him any longer, and was surrounded by other men. He needed to admit that her heart was only that small.

Khanh once reasoned that living selfishly, focusing on oneself rather than others, would be preferable. He thought success was only about fame and money, but when Phuong appeared, he realized that love affected him more than anything else.

His phone abruptly rang, startling him. It turned out to be Mac, an old friend of his. Mac was in trouble, according to the sound of gasping on the phone.

Khanh's guess was correct.

***

Khanh unlocked the car door and went forward, having just landed the car in the middle of the empty lot. The loan sharks proceeded to beat Mac in front of him until his face was bloated and blood was all over his clothes. Mac's face was etched with blows, cracked lips, and matted hair.

Khanh suddenly dropped a suitcase containing dozens of money piles on the ground as Mac was ready to be tormented with knuckles and the first teeth were broken.

Khanh was always this way; he was always distant, but he was always the one who showed up when people needed him. He had no idea how long he would be the "Buddha" in other people's lives. It appeared to be the fate that God had planned for him.

***

"Ring... ring... ring"

Khanh rang the doorbell repeatedly, but no one appeared to be home. While perplexed, Khanh was fortunate to discover a key to the gate in Mac's pocket. Khanh deftly grasped for the keys and then dragged Mac's 72 kg body into Mac's house.

Although Mac was not well enough to go home, he tried to persuade Khanh to take him home since he didn't want to be with strangers at the hospital any longer. Khanh was unable to leave Mac and simply departed. Although Mac was not in critical condition, his eyes, corners of his mouth, and entire body were plainly fatigued.

"Thank you so much, Khanh. You worked hard because of me." Mac responded. "I will work hard and find a way to repay you."

"How do you know if you are thankful? Taking care of yourself is what it means." Khanh gave a cool answer.

Khanh looked around after assisting Mac inside the room and tending to his brother on the bed. The wedding shot of Ly and Mac in the midst of the bedroom appeared to be quite cheerful. What if that love was as round as the one in the picture?

Khanh exhaled a sigh. He approached the window frame, lit a cigarette, and opened the window slightly to make the environment more comfortable.

"Why haven't you returned yet?" Khanh was startled when Mac spoke out. With a faint smile, he turned to face Mac.

"I took a breather before returning." You simply rest..."

"Are you... are you and Phuong dating?"

"How did you find out?" Khanh was taken aback. "It's still not an official relationship..."

"I caught her, and the other day you went to the movies..." Mac stepped in.

" ..."

"Did you really come to her because you liked Phuong?" I inquired.

"Don't be concerned..." Khanh paused for a few seconds. Naturally, it was. You don't even have the right to say anything because you abandoned her first. "Look after your family."

Mac remained silent. He didn't even look at Khanh. He turned around to the corner of the wall, leaving Khanh alone to gaze out the window at the unknown city. Mac examined the photograph Phuong had taken with the baby, as well as the photograph he had taken with Khanh many years before. Was it by chance that the fateful mole in the corner of that eye, between the boy and Khanh? Was there a secret here that he wasn't aware of?

Khanh rummaged through his pocket for a recording pen the other day while looking at the moonlight. He felt weirdly lonely while holding it in his palm. The freezing cold wind outside the window wiped away the tears welling up in the corners of his eyes.

His heart now felt so strangely because it had split into hundreds of small pieces.

April 2013

Apartment S, District 2

8.30 PM

Khanh stood in front of the apartment complex gate where Phuong lived. He had a stack of An's health documents, which he had just received this morning. Despite his mental preparation, he had never seen the border between truth and lying so thin.

He opened the phone screen and went through each old message Phuong had sent him to finish their "conversation." He didn't want it to end like this.

Khanh had many doubts about his feelings for Phuong, and he also desired a speedy connection. In the end, he was just like everyone else who had fallen in love. He sat alone on the sofa, drinking and simply reminiscing about their brief happy history together.

"I heard somewhere that people don't construct their lives on a few romantic recollections. You are aware of this. But I am unable to do so."

He still had a lot to say to Phuong. He had also not responded to her that he did not wish to end the relationship. He hadn't been able to get in touch with her for more than three months. She didn't respond to SMS, didn't answer the phone, and didn't do anything on social media.

He could just text her and wait tonight. She would have to meet him again before everything was totally resolved, as long as he waited for her a little longer and didn't give up.

He didn't want Phuong making such emotional choices. He'd made her favorite cuisine for dinner because he knew she wasn't in the habit of eating on time. Every day, the stomach ache wore her down to the point of withering.

It began to rain unexpectedly. Khanh stored the documents in his briefcase. Khanh looked about, but there was nowhere for him to stay. He rode his motorcycle today but forgot to bring his raincoat.

"There are only 15 minutes left! What on earth can this rain do to bring you down?" Khanh checked his watch, assuring himself that Phuong would arrive shortly.

Khanh clutched the food bag with both hands. He had to leave tomorrow for a two-week business trip. He had no idea what would happen during that time to transform Phuong. He needed to tell her what he was actually thinking as quickly as possible.

He couldn't afford to lose Phuong. Certainly not.

"What exactly are you doing here?"

Phuong's voice was heard from behind Khanh. She'd just gotten home from work, her entire body soaked from the rain.

Khanh's normal self-assurance and unapproachability is not as strong in front of Phuong today. For some reason, he wished to get rid of the arrogant appearance he had worked so hard to cultivate.

"I'd want to give this present." "Congratulations on your birthday!"

Khanh placed the food bag in Phuong's hand and prepared to go silently. Phuong grabbed his hand before he could react. She kissed him on the cheek.

"Don't leave me here right now... Not to mention that the rain will give you a cold!"

Khanh went completely still. Their lips met and became intertwined. Even though it was still raining severely, he felt horrible warmth while holding her. After months of tortured themselves with dozens of thoughts, that night was their first night together.

***

Chapter 11

"Isn't forgiveness the most terrible kind of vengeance?"

***** Six months later...**

October, 2013

XTV | Television station.

10.00 AM

Announcer: "Thank you for coming to today's inspirational talk show, writer Linh Phuong. Do you have anything to say to the show's audience?"

Linh Phuong:"I receive a lot of sharing and confiding from readers about love tales, good and wrong choices, regret or relief on social media and even in private mailboxes. relief following a relationship... I only have one thing to say: only you know what you truly require. Be more confident and aggressive in life by trusting your intuition and what your heart tells you."

"Cut! Excellent work." The show's end was signaled by the director.

Phuong laughed. She walked down to the stage, said farewell to the program team, and walked away. Everything appeared to be in place! Phuong was ecstatic, assuming to herself that "destiny" had suddenly manifested in front of her.

She also had a doctor's appointment this afternoon. She had been feeling tireder than usual for over three weeks.

Six months ago, Phuong and Khanh had just gotten back together. She had no idea why she had opted to reconcile with him. She just knew it was a feeling she couldn't put into words.

She remembered him and her, as well as the film team, carefully considering all of the footage and color of the film in just two weeks of traveling on a business trip. Khanh himself is a powerful figure in the worlds of showbiz and media; he partnered with the corporation to develop a marketing strategy for the picture to be successful with the audience, resulting in the film of the same name Phuong becoming a viable choice.

The film's earnings had surpassed 70 billion Vietnam Dong in just one month. Every program featured the "noses" of Khanh and Phuong, from the guest of honor to the speaker.

That was when Phuong realized her life had changed. At the very least, she was allowed to pursue her passion.

Khanh was responsible for everything. He was the one who made miracles happen in her life, allowing her dreams to take flight and come true.

Phuong examined the phone screen while driving to the hospital. She'd been living with Khanh for three months at this point. She also left her work at a media company to focus on her writing. Everything seemed to calm down. Strange dreams and hauntings from the past didn't bother her as much anymore.

Although not legally married, there didn't appear to be any distance between Phuong and Khanh. He and she shared some joyful times that she might never forget. Afternoons spent tasting the best ice cream in England, playing together in the lavender fields of France, or simply being in his arms, feeling the warmth of his lips while strolling down Le Duan street in the center of Saigon.

She desired to hold Khanh's hand and spend the rest of her life with him for the first time in her life. She desired to have a kid with him in order to commemorate her and his love with a fruitful outcome.

She was having a great time. She didn't have to show it; everyone could sense her pleasant spirit. Was love's power so tremendous that it made people's lives so sublime?

1.00 PM FV Hospital, District 7

"Doctor! Are there any results yet? "Did I catch a disease?" Phuong gazed worriedly at the doctor in front of her.

In contrast to Phuong's anxious demeanor, the doctor simply smiled and declared. "Congratulations to you! You're three weeks along! Take better care of your health starting now!"

Two beats... One beat... Her heart was racing faster than it had ever been. Was this true? Khanh would certainly jump for joy if he knew.

Phuong swiftly found the 1 key on the phone and dialed Khanh's number. She suddenly didn't want to call him for a few seconds. She planned to tell him when she got home. Only then would the happiness be complete.

She decided to say her goodbyes to the doctor, not forgetting to smile at him. She hadn't been able to put on such a complete smile in a long time. She wished to forget the painful recollections of the past. Because a fresh life had bloomed and instilled love in her once more.

6.00 PM

Today, Phuong decided to make a sour soup with stewed chicken that Khanh enjoyed. She rarely became involved in these issues on a daily basis. But because she loved him, she couldn't think of any excuse not to cook for him.

She dialed Khanh's number, but he did not answer. She had sent a message to Khanh, but he had not yet responded.

It was OK; he must be preoccupied with work. This would be the most amusing supper they'd ever had!

Phuong was ecstatic after eating the dish. She began to anticipate Khanh's return.

9.00 PM

The doorbell rang, jolting her awake. Khanh was unmistakably Phuong. He arrived later than usual today. It had to have happened out of nowhere! Phuong told herself this while staring boredly at the piles of cold food on the table.

Not wanting to keep Khanh waiting, Phuong opened the door, only to see a person bringing gifts to Khanh. Khanh, who frequently received presents from his partners because he was committed to assisting them, rarely calculated anything. Phuong adored Khanh because of his exceptional kindness. He made people feel comfortable and confident in his presence.

Phuong remained at the dinner table after receiving the present, waiting for Khanh. Because the work had recently gotten more intense, Khanh and her hardly spoke to each other. She wanted to take advantage of this opportunity to rekindle the "fire" of love in her and him.

Several minutes later. The doorbell rang once again. Khanh arrived home inebriated. Phuong assisted Khanh, but the strong odor of alcohol, mixed with the fact that she was pregnant, made her feel queasy. Khanh unconsciously threw his arms around her waist and kissed her on the lips.

"I adore you. I apologize for everything ". Khanh had hardly done speaking when he collapsed. Khanh's employment required him to frequently meet his partners and attend gatherings like this.

She sat down beside Khanh. She felt sorry for him. But her heart was filled with an inexplicable sense of anguish for some reason.

***

After a week...

Khanh's house

10.00 PM

It was the ninth day after Phuong discovered she was pregnant. She couldn't keep her happiness from Khanh any longer.

Khanh grew further and further away from her every day. He was on his way to Hanoi airport after a drunken night the night before to work for more than a week before returning. He simply left a sheet of paper in front of the fridge with the message, "Please take care of your health." You're always so busy these days!" then proceeded straight.

Phuong wasn't frightened or thinking too much, but she had the impression that there was an invisible barrier between her and Khanh. She didn't get it. Things were still going swimmingly. Phuong's name, appearance, and the number of persons who ordered her scripts remained consistent. As for Khanh, he was now working with more partners, had more scripts to manage, and his communication and branding work had become denser and more complicated. But what if the company was suffering a significant difficulty or his family was hiding anything from her?

Khanh, Phuong suddenly remembered, never mentioned his family.

Phuong took her antidepressant. She struggled for a long time to break the habit of utilizing this medicine whenever something went wrong. It was a small amount of nervous anxiety she had to pay for her current serene life.

Phuong sat alone at the table, sipping some juice. Phuong commented as he watched Khanh gently enter the house and proceed straight to the stairs:

"Did you get drunk today again?"

"No." Khanh responded quickly. "Do you have anything you wish to tell me?"

"I won't inquire why you don't kiss me on the cheek as you used to. Back in the day, I could tell when you were happy or unhappy by looking into your eyes, so I could be at your side and share. And now I'm at a loss..."

"... Let's discuss this tomorrow; I'm a little fatigued today..."

"How long will you hide from me?" You don't even look at my face anymore..."

Khanh accidently laughed out loud after not letting Phuong complete saying. His smile conveyed happiness, grief, and wonder, all of which he had worked hard to conceal for so long. He stretched out instinctively and knocked over a valuable vase on a nearby shelf. He hurled the fragile stuff in the house on the ground one by one. Everything broke. Phuong screamed in terror at Khanh's deeds.

"Are you not my wife? We simply coexist." Khanh locked his gaze on Phuong's. "What gives you the right to question me?"

"I..." Phuong's eyes were wide with surprise and fear.

"You're quite astute." Khanh grinned. "You used to belong to my father, but now you're mine."

"What is your father's name?" Phuong couldn't disguise her awe. Phuong felt shocked, as if something had flashed across her thoughts. "You mentioned your father died a long time ago..."

"Do you remember Mr. Vu Huy Khiem from ten years ago?"

"..."

"He is my father, the man who provided for you and was murdered by you."

"Didn't you already know...?" Phuong tried to mask her anguish with her labored breathing. "But you... you look nothing like your father..."

"I lost my face in a traffic accident that year, and I never imagined I'd be able to receive another face after so many agonizing procedures."

"..."

"However, the mole under my eye remains. "Take a close look!" Khanh threw the photograph he had taken with his father to the ground. Phuong bent down carefully to take it up. Her entire body became really heated. Even though she was the culprit that year, she felt like a victim.

"I used to think I was in love with you. How many times in my life have I begged you to let me love you, to let the love in me forgive you... But the closer I get to you, the more I notice my father's silhouette..."

"Might it be... in the first place... could it be you...?" Phuong has one hand on the table and the other on her stomach. The stomach discomfort appeared whenever she was anxious, making her feel miserable.

"Get up! Do you believe in the existence of "accident" or "destiny" in this world?

" ... "

"Why did I appear when you needed me the most? Why did I set up a shop in the same building as you? Why did I volunteer to work with you and help you become the person you are now? Why would I offer myself to you and build something called "family"?

" ... ".

"I've been keeping tabs on your every action..." Khanh made a chirp. "I want to give you everything and take everything away from you." I want you to realize that happiness is difficult to attain, but easy to lose..."

" ... "

"Don't trust anyone in this world.Who would have guessed that a successful screenwriter like you could so callously murder the person who had supplied for you and raised you for a while?"

Khanh took a pen from his pocket and began recording. An and Phuong's voices were clearly heard in the tape ten years ago, which surprised Phuong.

"How long am I going to put up with this? I don't want to maintain this repulsive object any longer. I don't want you to retain it either."

Khanh concealed his grief in a harsh sob as he placed the recording pen on the table. He dashed out of the house, driving the Ducati without looking back.

Phuong leaned on the chair's armrest. Her heart was heavy and hurting. She was cold. Her hand brushed the scorching tears from the corner of her eye, some of which spilled onto her calloused hand. She closed her eyes and let the pleasant memories flood back to her mind.

She wanted nothing more than to wish the two had never met... She had lost not just love, but also hope.

***

"Please assist me in getting out of this gloomy area."
If this is a dream, please assist me in waking up as soon as possible.
Please tell me it's all a lie.
Please tell me, please tell me, and then I shall live..." (*)

(*) Lyrics to "Sick Enough to Die"

Khanh switched the switch, hit the Ducati's start button, heard the engine roar, and drove off to the southern highway. He turned the headphones up to maximum volume. He wanted to get out of Saigon, to bury all the memories he had with Phuong.

He was weak and vulnerable. He sped down the highway, tempting fate and ignoring fate. He couldn't hear her voice in his ear any longer. He wished to cast the past into the abyss.

Khanh was the one who injured Phuong. He was the one who duped Phuong.

Khanh had told himself numerous times that he was a coward. He used to merely want to play with her, to handcuff her and take her to the prison as soon as possible.

Khanh's hand was responsible for arranging a magical love in the eyes of many individuals. He studied and learnt everything he could about the previous case from the press, until he recognized Phuong - An's best friend - in a photo taken with An in the appeal court that year. He couldn't deal with An directly since he didn't have enough proof to declare that the previous tale was not convincing enough.

He made the decision to seek Phuong for more information. He began following her the moment she picked up An from the prison. He made the decision to house the company's headquarters in the same building where she worked. He followed her home from work every time. He was in the bar and was watching her from a distance. When Phuong and An's familiar voices arrived on the audio, he realized everything. He confided in and talked with Mac to learn more about her so he could simply approach her. He approached An and slept with Ha in order to conveniently obtain proof against her and reveal her secret.

So, what did he end up with? A bloody recording pen, a health certificate attesting to An's good health with few evidence of methamphetamine use, a picture Phuong took with her child - the ill-fated child - and confirmation that the infant was his father's son.

Khanh laughed, and his chest tightened.

He recalled his 19th birthday, when he had just survived a horrible truck accident in Hanoi. His transformation from a gorgeous man to a horrible creature has caused others to gradually distance himself. He stayed indoors all day, only venturing out into the street when it got dark. He contemplated dying several times in his anguish. But when confronted with reality, with his aged mother still struggling daily with groceries to support him, he still wanted to live and secretly hopes he could modify his face and start over. His mother's sole hope was in him. He didn't want her to cry for him any longer.

Khanh's narrative made the physicians' hearts melt two years later, when attending a reality TV show on the city's television station, and they decided to grant him a seat as a new face. A new life had opened up for him, one that was not only full of opportunity because of his good looks and talents, but also allowed old hatreds to sneak back into his heart.

He was still in shock at what had happened to his father. He had lost all faith in fairness. He convinced himself that if each person did not find a way to fight for himself, no one else would.

Then he started looking into the relationship between An, Phuong, and other unusual characters. So much danger, so much decay in their spirits. It didn't take him long to win their hearts, because they, like him, craved for truth in the depths of their souls.

"The depths of the soul... How deep does it go? Is it feasible to proceed all the way to the end?"

When he decided to confront Phuong and exact revenge on her, he had no idea that his heart would remain with her ever since. When they were both at the pinnacle of their renown, he and she had moments of success. He accompanied her to horizons only the two of them knew about.

He wanted to do his best for her because he once loved her. Because he knew that if her background was uncovered, she would no longer be able to begin her profession.

And if she discovered he was the son of a guy who had been badly injured by her, she would never be able to face him again.

He wanted her to be the one to make her own decisions about everything that transpired in her life. He remembered that whenever he heard her say his name, he forgot about everything.

He stopped smoking, drinking heavily, and engaging in long drinking sessions with his companion as a result of her influence.

Because of her, he felt more empathy and compassion for everyone.

He was willing to go to any length for her.

He desired to be with her indefinitely. Then he remembered he had a grudge against someone. That caused him to suffer. As a result, he was unable to relax when confronted with his father.

He acknowledged being terrified. He didn't want to spend his life like this any longer. He was concerned that the time they had spent together would soon come to an end.

He wanted her to comprehend what she had done, what she had hidden.

Was it true that the most agonizing vengeance is forgiveness?

***

An returned home. He opened the door to the room, as usual pressing the switch to turn on the electricity.

Ann was taken aback. Phuong had been missing from this flat for three months but had reappeared in front of him. She was inebriated, dressed sloppily, her hair drooping, and resting on the living room floor.

"You always know how to motivate others, that's what I appreciate about you!" recalled Phuong. But An's innocent ability that day seemed to have died.

"No worries. Phuong, An has arrived!" An felt like an empty promiseer every time he repeated that remark with Phuong. There was obviously nothing he could do. He obviously couldn't improve Phuong. He was just standing there, waiting for Phuong to return to him, even though he knew it would only happen when Phuong needed him.

"Khanh... He knew everything about us that year, An..."

"How could..."

"You know, not only did I accidently kill that man that year... I also had a child with him..."

"...How come Phuong didn't inform An sooner?"

"Many times, I imagined I'd be able to disregard everything and live quietly because of the child... I attempted to give birth to and raise it... 5 years passed in peace... When I was picking up my child from school, I was irresponsible and my son was involved in a traffic accident..."

"..."

"I began there and began all over again... I assumed I couldn't forget... Until I reconnected with Khanh and had a child with him..."

"..."

"But he is the son of the man Phuong met 10 years ago."

"..."

"An, am I genuinely unworthy of genuine love?"

An was stunned for quite some time. The heart felt befuddled and dumbfounded. He embraced Phuong. In the past, Phuong was extremely difficult to overcome. If it hadn't been for her father's death and the lack of assistance, Phuong would not have been readily deterred by a man her father's age from having more money to support such a desire.

How could An forget the night Phuong cried out to An? She endured the humiliation of being degraded by a man her father's age? He even treated her like a toy, ruthlessly beating her.

Phuong didn't intend to do so. It was just a mistake.

Was there a night in the last 10 years when Phuong actually slept? Was there ever a time when she didn't have pity on herself and the buddy who gave up her youth for her?

How could Phuong return to his previous life calmly? She couldn't do it. An, on the other hand, could not bear the thought of Phuong suffering in prison.

An didn't believe it; he'd rather have blood on his hands.

An opted to take the blame for the crime instead of Phuong.

An then proceeded to destroy the camera from outside the gate of that man's property, removed all traces of everything relating to Phuong's image, and replaced it on the ashtray and surrounding objects with all of An's fingerprints around. An decided to replace Phuong as the shocking underage killer that year. An also urged Phuong to fabricate a bogus medical certificate to demonstrate that he was conducting the crime in a psychotic state. The police and the court saw evidence of ashtrays, indications of methamphetamine, and a direct confession of wanting to rob a killer with fifty million dollars taken from Mr. Huy Khiem's locker as a very credible cause. The verdict may convict An.

An had recently been drifting with an uncertain future, no dreams, no notion what he wanted, and no idea what was truly required. If An couldn't find something to live for, Phuong had a long road ahead of him.

An decided to make a stand-in for himself and Phuong. It was the best thing he could do right now for the person he cared about.

An understood he was alone throughout the most trying and depressing time. Alone when leaving love, leaving relatives who were grandmothers in the sunny and breezy countryside of Quang Nam. Stand alone in the face of strangers' harshness. When the police officers tried to frighten and abuse An, he was alone.

But, An reasoned, if Phuong had to live behind these bars, An would have suffered more pain than the rest of them.

Chapter 12

"Thank you for giving me such a fleeting moment of happiness and transporting me to a world I had no idea existed."

***

10 a.m., October 2013

Cafe Nest

Linh Phuong, the "screenwriter wizard," would hold a press conference to unveil the film.

Nest Cafe's romantic golden light shone down into the space, making the press conference feel especially snug and elegant. Journalists and guests gradually arrived. The auditorium immediately became full.

Speaking to the MC at the press conference with the directors and actresses, Phuong expressed her dissatisfaction with having to attend this media circus, but could she do otherwise when she had to show up everywhere she went and compete with a slew of new factors?

She couldn't get out of her fight with Khanh last night. She should have canceled this morning's press conference. But she couldn't break the promise she made to Khanh, the pledge to work "to the point" in any situation.

She still clutched her recording pen from the day before. She couldn't get the snapshot with the father and son's smile out of her head.

She was not furious with Khanh, nor did she forget to thank Khanh; she simply did not dare to confront the man she had affections for until it was too late.

Khanh, the man who gave her a "spark of love," she couldn't forget. It was something she didn't think would happen again in her life. He offered her a little moment of delight before whisking her away to a world she had never experienced. It turned out that she was finally able to transform the feeling known as love for him. She should have been the happiest lady on the planet.

Each passing instant made her joyful, but it also wounded her. She was dubious, perhaps believing that because she was strong, she would never be able to create the feeling that people want to protect her like any other women.

Her life had taught her to be wary of men. Even if he was reassuring in certain ways, she couldn't accept him. As a result, none of her love stories have had a future.

She was used to the fact that she would never be surrounded by a fairy or a Buddha. She was always certain that only she could save herself.

But, without Khanh, Phuong was definitely alone.

In love, Phuong told herself, there were things she peculated on based on what she knew, but there were things the other side never voiced what they thought. So, for better or worse, only time would tell.

Everyone thought they were approaching each other, yet they never met. As a result, the two split up since they didn't believe it was the happiness they deserved.

She realized the relationship between Khanh and her was ended. Khanh taught her that the past might be pleasant memories, but that this was not the case. She should have understood to cherish him from the beginning, not when it slipped from her grasp and she regretted going to find it.

Phuong believed she knew everything. But she had no idea that at the far end of the auditorium, a familiar man in spectacles and a white shirt was staring at her with burning eyelids. He could have gone straight to the front of the stands, accusing this woman of betraying his sentiments after murdering his father twelve years before, but he didn't.

***

Apartment S, District 2

2.00 PM

Phuong entered the restroom. She turned the faucet as high as she could while locking the door to the left. As if she wished to bury the previous half-awake days, she plunged herself in the rising water that filled the tub, the hot smoke slowly emitting.

She gazed at herself in the mirror on the other side. With sad eyes, the old 15-year-old girl looked at herself. "What exactly are you doing? What exactly are you doing? Why should I be sad?" Her thoughts were loaded with regrets from the past.

Since Phuong's first child died at the time, she has never ceased paying weekly visits to the cemetery, nor has the baby's grin stopped haunting her nightmares. Her internal anguish was palpable.

She had been so odd, so insane, that no one dared to approach her.

Love, it was commonly claimed, was a selfless giving. Phuong didn't need love; she only needed a partner who respected and supported her, but was it so difficult?

She undoubtedly felt joy again throughout her days of knowing Khanh. Even though Phuong had approached Khanh from the first time she saw him enter the studio in the same building, only to become an editor, it had been a long time since she'd found herself smiling so carelessly. She tried everything, inadvertently noticed the phrase Tinder, then collided into each other from the elevator door and from working late at the office.

Phuong was aware that she had stimulated Khanh's need to please herself, owing to her selfish attitude and habit of taking advantage of her. Attempting to seduce a man for both love and money. But she couldn't "seduce" herself out of her sorrow.

Obviously, Phuong couldn't forget the bloody hand for a man, couldn't ignore the fact that she killed him even if it was only manslaughter. Getting to know and like Khanh - living in harmony with a man's body as delicate as hers wounded both of them but couldn't change anything.

When Phuong calculated and thought so much, she recognized that it was only because she still kept the concept that she would pursue a romantic love, a pure love without profit. Though she understood, she would continue to feel tormented and shattered as long as she tried to replace the void in her heart with someone else's heart.

After several injuries, her heart remained pure and innocent. She couldn't understand why she chose to live in those uncertain days after so many blunders.

Phuong let the salty tears in her eyes mix with the water. She went out of the tub, dried her hair, put on a lovely black shirt, and began writing her ten-year-old confessions. She burst into tears as a wave raced through her.

Phuong had to pay a debt, a selfless love, sooner or later.

***

In the next 4 years...

Quang Nam's Cua Dai Beach

4.00 PM

Phuong grabbed a few shots with his phone while watching the toddler play with friends on the sand. Children around the age of four or five, such as Phuong's son, always amused her. Every time she looked at her child, she was distracted by her phone's wallpaper - Khanh. The baby had a face, a smile, and eyes. It was like seeing him when she saw her child. That was simply too much for her heart to endure.

She missed Khanh in a way that could not be expressed in words. In her opinion, Khanh was the one who brought her the best times.

She and Khanh have not spoken to each other in a long time.

Phuong had been gone from that dark mansion for four years. Four years had gone since she decided to return to the distant countryside of Quang Nam, rent a house, and live alone with her newborn child.

An's support was always present on Phuong's side, even from a distance.

Phuong exclusively exchanged images and information on the infant with An via text messages, emails, and a few social networking sites that year. Phuong did not reveal the baby's existence or whereabouts, despite the fact that the baby's name was revealed to Khanh.

Thanh Nhan was the name she gave to her child. Because she want that he grow up to be a good person.

Phuong turned to face An. They were sitting next to one other in a toad shop on the seashore, saying things they would never tell anyone.

"Have you given it much thought?" An lit a cigarette and asked Phuong patiently.

"Sure. I completed everything. I could finally relax! I have to pay this debt anyway!"

"However, you must guarantee that you would always look after yourself."

"I said I would." Phuong laughed. "Thank you for driving me and Thanh Nhan to this beach today to view the sunset one more time."

"That year, I realized that my sacrifice for you was correct. Because your future was still bright, your dream was my delight, and you...were the person I used to love."

" ... "

"Please contact Khanh, Phuong. Khanh is entitled to know everything about the child and everything you have been through... And let Khanh make Thanh Nhan's life better."

An turned to face Phuong. Phuong responded with tears in her eyes. Phuong placed her head on An's shoulder, enjoying the gorgeous sunset on the sea today. They began talking about their old recollections once more. An was the kind of buddy Phuong knew she'd never have again in her life.

They sat close because they knew they could rely on one another. Because there was the same pain in their eyes, which not everyone could understand.

Chapter 13

"When did we become so selfish to the point of fear?"

Since when was love in us merely a "sufficient condition," rather than a "required condition" as it was previously?"

In November of 2017,

The very first day...

Phuong was shocked when she looked through the little window at the glimmer of light. The sky turned out to be already bright. She shrank when she realized she was no longer in the room with the familiar gray walls.

She hadn't had to wake up in a long time to apply powder, eyeliner, and lipstick to freshen up. In this frigid cage, she was laying next to strangers.

They were individuals who didn't care how famous she was; all they wanted to know was that when she came here, she was their "kind," or just inferior.

Phuong's lips pursed.For the "thirsty news" days, celebrity misery was always a rich lure for journalists.

THE MOST RECOGNIZED SCREENWRITER IN VIETNAM HAS UNEXPECTEDLY CONFESSED.

AT THE AGE OF 15, A PROMINENT YOUNG FEMALE SCREENWRITER UNEXPECTEDLY UNCOVERED HER TRAGIC HISTORY.

Phuong burst out laughing. Because she had resolved to restart her life. She was "dead" a long time ago in the past.

Phuong had a "meeting" with her old assistant and An, her greatest friend in life, this morning. Ha and An couldn't help but feel sad when they saw Phuong, emaciated and thin with prison life:

"I didn't think you'd be able to live here, boss!"

"I'm no longer your boss. Aren't you scared of me?"

"How can I be terrified of you? I'll never find a manager who will take me out to dine as a probationer. There's just you."

"Really? It's been a long time, yet I recall it vividly." Phuong burst out laughing.

"Yes".

The talk abruptly came to a halt. Ha turned to face An. An and Phuong exchanged glances without saying anything. Not allowing "dead time" to pass, Ha stated first:

"When you announced your resignation, I assumed you were going to concentrate on becoming a screenwriter. But I didn't believe another day like this would come..."

"But I'm such a moron, aren't I?" I could still bury everything, survive, and rebuild my life..."

"But if you don't admit it, you won't be able to grin as easily as you do today..." An unintended let go, a sad and encouraging smile at Phuong.

"...". When Phuong stared at An, tears streamed down her cheeks.

"You will never choose to flee since you are Phuong, my boss..." Ha's eyes were fixed on something. "I apologize for my folly."

" ... "

"Because of you, I know that life is meaningless without passion." I recently resigned my job and opened my favorite coffee business with An. At the bar, I also sing."

Ha discreetly smiled and handed Phuong an instax photo of An and Ha standing in front of the cafe. Phuong smiled as he glanced at the photo, knowing that each of them had discovered their genuine passion and purpose in life.

It was said by the eyes that were both looking at Phuong at the time.

2nd day...

I was confident that this dashing white shirt would see me through the day.

This was also the day four years ago that Ly and I agreed to stop being together and stop viewing each other.

When the divorce trial ended four years ago, the road was flooded. I crouched on the cold porch, waiting for the taxi, even though I had no idea where I was going.

Although there was no longer love, I couldn't deny what was between me and Ly. I was still attempting to repay Khanh for the money I owed him when I decided to work numerous jobs at the same time.

Ly didn't lose while dating other young guys, not thinking about our children, ever since I established to myself that my feelings were over. Not to add that I couldn't forgive Ly for my brutal treatment of Phuong. However, I was suddenly a lonely man with no one around.

First and foremost, I would fulfill my role as a father. In front of the court, I made the decision to take custody of the children. My daughter, Bao Anh, was now four years old. Every day, seeing her smile, cuddle, and inquire about her feelings makes me happy.

Today, while I sat in a taxi, watching the white rain obscure all the images of bystanders, I burst out laughing because life was a fantasy. I only woke up when a certain milestone unexpectedly blocked my path. However, the emotion left behind was frequently nothing but emptiness. I reached out with my palm for the speck of rain on the car door, having awoken, but the stars surrounding me were only a gray sky, chilly and empty raindrops.

My life used to be extremely tranquil, but after meeting Phuong, everything fell apart. But I had to acknowledge something: how nice would it be if I didn't have that type of tranquility to come to Phuong and steal her heart? And now that Phuong's love for me was over, what did I have to fight for?

This life seemed to have a deeper purpose that I couldn't fathom. Obviously, I had no understanding and no control over anything. I was mistaken in expecting that Phuong would always be waiting for me.

Even after learning that Phuong had surrendered, committed manslaughter, and that the infant in the photograph was her ill-fated son, I was never disgusted with her. As I grew older, I discovered that it was usual for people to be less than they appeared to be. This life was not always as great as we assumed

I still thought the narrative of Phuong and Khanh was a never-ending grace. But perhaps I was the most foolish and simple individual in the world when I thought hatred could be cured by evaporating on its own without any sacrifice.

I sat across from Phuong, my hand stroking her face through the glass pane. My life was full of flavor once more, and my feelings were as intense as the first time I met her. My heart felt weirdly precious every time I saw Phuong smile. My love was like a boomerang, returning me to the past so that I might love Phuong once more.

But maybe I was the only one who felt that way just now. Phuong had waited much too long for my return. That was four years ago. There were silences, gloomy periods, and questions I never dared to ask for fear of having to know the answer. But, in the lack of evidence or doubt, weren't we free to believe whatever we wanted?

"How are you feeling these days?"

"I'm still fine, still smiling regardless of what life was like previously."

"Yes. I wanted to touch you from the moment I saw you, but I only dared to keep my distance."

"Did you believe that once you returned to Saigon, everything would be fine as long as you grew more mature and successful?"

"..."

"Even if you improve, there will always be someone better than you. If you are better, someone will be better than you. You only lose my respect and trust... I'm not determined or daring enough to do anything else."

"I know I done things involving you..."

"I never anticipate when I will fall in love, so why is it that I can't find someone like that to be with for the rest of my life?"

"As a matter of fact, anyone who loves you will always calculate"...

"..."

"However, rather than thinking about themselves, they will think about the needs of others..."

"Is that correct...? Only now did I realize... Anyway, I appreciate you coming into my life."

I gave Phuong a friendly smile. That was how humans were. People overlooked love while it was present. When love got out of hand, people began to seek them out in their dreams.

Phuong was my favorite when she was 22. Phuong was as innocent and frail as a blank sheet of paper at the moment. Phuong's presence in my life at the time was like a ray of brightness in the midst of dark days.

Perhaps they were correct, fate intervened.

Perhaps they were correct; fate intervened when we least expected it.

Could I correct my youth's faults in a single day?

3rd day...

Khanh had always believed that she made the right decision for everyone. But he didn't realize that everyone had a different life situation and learned various lessons, thus his choice would never be the best for others. In this world, no one was the same, no one understood anyone, but they were the only ones who made decisions without regret.

Khanh couldn't believe it had been four years since he had visited his father's cemetery. Even though he knew that if he didn't accept it, nothing would change.

But his perspective had shifted.

He had awoken the sleeping past. Just because he couldn't forgive. Just because he didn't trust what they said: "Forgiveness says one thing: I was right, and you were wrong."

And he wanted to be as calm as possible every time he saw Phuong.

Why was it so difficult for him to comprehend forgiveness?

Why was sympathy such a trickle in his heart?

Holding the baby's little hand, he let his sorrows flow back in time. The boy smiled at him. The boy resembled him down to the wrinkles in his eyes, the bridge of his nose, and the shape of his lips. Because the boy's name was Thanh Nhan, he had to finally know and feel all the bitterness in order to become a person.

It was time for him to start anew and be honest to himself. He fell in love with someone he shouldn't have. He made mistakes. He couldn't accept it. But he couldn't run away forever.

"We will reap what we have sown, sooner or later. We cannot fight the trugic flow of events in life. We believe we have the right to choose, but those pathways have always been aimed at us".

Khanh gazed at the woman in front of him. She wasn't wearing makeup today. Her eyes remained large, her complexion remained dazzling white, and only her lips were somewhat pale. Was she awake enough in this environment to always seem as gorgeous as the day she first met four years ago?

He had never imagined that he and she could communicate so coldly.

How can two individuals who used to hold each other and feel each other's breath treat each other like strangers?

"Do we have anything to discuss?"

"I haven't talked to you much yet..."

"Take excellent care of Thanh Nhan!"

"Yes. He's alone outside, playing Yoyo..."

"Aren't you supposed to go to work today?"

"My life is more than just work."

"So, how come I didn't realize you were obsessed with business when we first met?" You just saw me on weekends back then?"

"You are as well. You also indicated that every time we met, a few hours were sufficient. Wasn't it supposed to be possible to strike a balance between love and work...?"

"Is that, by the way, love?"

After seeing Phuong's profound smile, Khanh's eyes were tired. He had no idea what was going on inside of him.

He used to believe that love entailed making sacrifices for one another, making one another feel at ease and glad to be around; yet, to be honest, he didn't know how to accomplish those things either. He merely wanted to live as himself, to find a puzzle piece who shared his thoughts so that both of them could be at ease.

"How come you didn't tell me you had a child with me? If you'd told me back then, maybe it wouldn't have come to this..."

'Because you didn't allow a single moment of stillness for me that night... At the moment, all I wanted to do was ask you to listen to me even once..."

"..."

"Then I ask myself, is it acceptable with you, even if only for a moment?"

"..."

"... Look after Thanh Nhan. Because that is what distinguishes us as having a wonderful time."

Khanh remained silent. He instantly averted his gaze. The spectacles hid the hot tears that streamed down his cheeks. Khanh clearly couldn't control his feelings. He used to tell himself that his life was not complicated, but it was. Now that he understood, the vibrations from his own heart overtook reason once again.

Khanh never wanted to see her sorrowful eyes and confident smile again.

Khanh regretted having just passed through the prison door. He wished he was in the middle of nowhere so he could drown out his pain right now.

Phuong wiped the tears that had fallen on her eyelids with her hand. She realized it was time to get rid of the agony, to get rid of the shadow of the past, to get away from her own life.

She used to live in this manner. She would sooner inflict pain on others than feel abandoned.

When did she start living such a terrifyingly selfish life? Since when was her love merely a "sufficient condition," rather than a "required requirement" as it had previously been?

Why should she wait until she was separated, when she had lost something, to express her feelings?

***

Outside the prison, Thanh Nhan was mischievously playing Yoyo. The child had no idea what his father was up to; all he knew was that he was visiting a friend. His mother had promised to return to him after a certain period of time the day before. He realized that Mom was focused with work and had a lot on her plate. Without a certain, he would not have asked and wondered as much as his kindergarten peers. Because his name was Thanh Nhan, and he was always more knowledgeable than others. His mother had told him to live this way.

The child spotted a friend his own age playing Yoyo while traveling and practicing each method of winding Yoyo. It was a little boy clothed in a vintage white pullover and blue sweatpants. Their upper eyelids were both covered in moles. Thanh Nhan was about to start a conversation with this friend when his father interrupted him from behind, causing the boy to turn his head in surprise:

"Please return, son. I've made delightful treats that you're sure to adore!"

"Yes."

Despite his father's worries, Thanh Nhan boarded the car parked in front of the gate and bid farewell to his little companion.

The boy, dressed in a white sweater and blue tracksuit, smiled quietly as he watched the car drive further and further away on the road, as if anticipating a day like today. He vanished in an instant, leaving just a few shimmering dust imprints...

***

Listen to me while it's still not over...
Listen to me when our efforts are insufficient...
When my eyes still make you nostalgic, listen to me...

THE END